# FURTHER *Curriculum Bank* ACTIVITIES

# WRITING

## KEY STAGE TWO / SCOTTISH LEVELS C–E

**DAVID WAUGH**

**Published by Scholastic Ltd,**
Villiers House,
Clarendon Avenue,
Leamington Spa,
Warwickshire CV32 5PR
Text © David Waugh
© 2000  Scholastic Ltd
1234567890 0123456789

Author
**David Waugh**

Editor
**Clare Gallaher**

Assistant editor
**Clare Miller**

Series designer
**Rachel Warner**

Designer
**Rachael Hammond/Paul Cheshire**

Illustrations
**Peter Stevenson**

Cover illustration
**Lesley Saddington**

Scottish 5–14 links
**Margaret Scott and Susan Gow**

British Library Cataloguing-in-Publication Data
A catalogue record for this book is available from
the British Library.

ISBN 0-590-53980-9

# Contents

# Introduction

Welcome to *Further Curriculum Bank Writing* (Key Stage 2/Scottish Levels C–E). This book provides a bank of activities which can be used as part of a scheme of work for English, and complements those which appear in the original book, *Curriculum Bank Writing*.

The book is divided into three sections: 'Imaginative writing', 'Non-fiction writing' and 'Language study'. Photocopiable sheets are provided to support many of the lessons and these may be adapted to meet the particular needs of the children in your class.

Most of the lesson plans include suggestions for adaptation for Literacy Hour work. There is a strong emphasis upon the discussion of the content of texts as well as the ways in which they are presented. Many of the activities could be started as part of the Literacy Hour and then be continued to provide opportunities for extended writing. While it is important that children study texts closely and discuss vocabulary and grammar, it is also vital that they be given opportunities to write at length and to explore their use of written language. The activities should not, therefore, be used simply as Literacy Hours and opportunities should be sought for extended writing at other times.

Where suggestions are made for Literacy Hour work, the year and term in which this might most appropriately be done is shown. However, most lessons can easily be adapted to meet the needs of classes throughout the seven to eleven age range, and the year and term should be regarded only as an indication and should not be adhered to rigidly.

Throughout the book, technical vocabulary is used when appropriate. Teachers should not be afraid of using the correct terminology when discussing language with children. An understanding of terms such as *adverb, tense* and *syllable* will enable children to discuss their writing and other people's more easily.

Many of the activities are designed to involve children working either independently or in pairs. Co-operative work can enable children to discuss vocabulary choices and phrasing as well as a sharing of ideas for content. On some occasions children might be asked to produce joint pieces of writing, while on others they could be asked to write independently and then show their work to a writing partner. This allows them to comment on each other's work and to suggest ideas for improvement. Discussing writing in this way provides an incentive for children to think carefully about what they and others have written and enables them to have the kind of feedback which published authors receive.

Writing should be an enjoyable activity and should not be confined to completing exercises and writing short pieces, although each of these has a place in the primary classroom. Children need time to draft, edit and revise work and to hone it until they can present it to others and feel proud of it. This will only happen if they are given extended opportunities for writing and are provided with real audiences for what they have written.

All of the activities have been extensively trialled in schools and then modified and revised where necessary. We hope that your pupils will enjoy them as much as others have.

**Lesson plans**

Detailed lesson plans, under clear headings, are given for each activity and provide material for immediate implementation in the classroom. The structure for each activity is as follows.

### Activity title box

The box at the beginning of each activity outlines the following key aspects:

▲ *Learning objective.* The learning objectives break down aspects of the programmes of study for English into manageable teaching and learning chunks. They can easily be referenced to the National Curriculum for England and Wales and the Scottish National Guidelines 5–14 by using the overview grid on pages 7–12.

▲ *Class organization/Likely duration.* The icons ✝✝ and 🕐 indicate the suggested group sizes for each activity and the approximate amount of time required to complete it.

### Previous skills/knowledge needed

This section gives information when it is necessary for the children to have acquired specific knowledge or skills prior to carrying out the activity.

### Key background information

This outlines the areas of study covered by each activity and gives a general background to the particular topic or theme, outlining the basic skills that will be developed and the way in which the activity will address the children's learning.

*Literacy Hour:* this section shows how the lesson could form part of a series of Literacy Hours and suggests the year and term for which such lessons might be most appropriate.

### Preparation

Advice is given when it is necessary for the teacher to prime the pupils for the activity, to prepare materials or to set up a display or activity ahead of time.

### Resources needed

All materials needed to carry out the activity, including photocopiable pages, are listed here.

### What to do

Clear step-by-step instructions are provided for carrying out the activity. These include (where appropriate) suitable questions for the teacher to ask the children in order to help instigate discussion and stimulate a high quality of writing.

### Suggestion(s) for extension/support

In these sections, ways of providing differentiation are suggested.

### Assessment opportunities

Where appropriate, opportunities for ongoing teacher assessment of the children's work during or after the activity are highlighted.

### Opportunities for IT

Where relevant IT work would strengthen an activity, appropriate possibilities are outlined.

### Display ideas

Where they are relevant and innovative, display ideas are incorporated into the activity plans, perhaps illustrated with examples.

### Other aspects of the English PoS covered

Inevitably, as all areas of English are interrelated, activities will cover aspects of the programmes of study in other areas of the English curriculum. These links are highlighted under this heading.

### Reference to photocopiable sheets

Photocopiable activity sheets are provided for use with particular activities. Small reproductions of these are included in the appropriate lesson plans, together with notes on their use and, if appropriate, suggested answers to questions.

# Overview Grid

This grid helps you to track the coverage of the Writing part of the Programme of Study for English at Key Stage 2, or the Scottish National Guidelines for English Language 5–14 at Levels C–E, offered by the activities in this book. For each activity, the relevant statements from the National Curriculum for England and Wales and the Scottish 5–14 Guidelines are indicated (the latter references are given in italics).

Most of the activities in this book are linked to the Curriculum Bank for Writing at Key Stage 2/Scottish Levels C–E. These links are indicated by footnotes below the relevant activities.

| ACTIVITY TITLE | LEARNING OBJECTIVE | POS/AO | NLS | CONTENT | PAGE |
|---|---|---|---|---|---|
| **IMAGINATIVE WRITING** | | | | | |
| **The broken window** | To write additional text in the style of an author, after attempting to use the style to create a story opening. | 2b. *Imaginative writing: Level C.* | Y5 T3 | Discussing texts and then writing in a similar style to an established author. Individual or group writing based upon texts provided. | 13 |
| **What happened next? page 30** | | | | | |
| **Girls don't play football** | To write persuasively | 1b, c; 2a. *As above.* | Y5 T3 | Persuasive writing. Individuals, pairs and groups. | 15 |
| **It's not fair! page 100** | | | | | |
| **The lion poems** | To use experience of published texts to help structure their own writing. To appreciate that different graphemes can represent the same phoneme. | 1c; 2b. *As above.* | Y6 T2 or Y5 T2 | Looking at two stories in poetic form and writing a story poem on a similar theme. Individual or paired work. | 16 |
| **Cautionary tales, page 34** | | | | | |
| **Dear Jack** | To write an explanation in role for an audience. To write an informal letter. | 1b, c. *Functional writing: Level C.* | Y5 T3 | Writing a letter from the character Jack, who appears in *Jack and the Beanstalk*, in response to a letter from the Giant. Individual work. | 17 |
| **Nursery stories for younger children, page 36** | | | | | |
| **Imaginary dialogue** | To use speech marks accurately in imaginative writing. | 1b, c; 2c. *Imaginative writing: Level D.* | Y5 T1 | Writing an imaginary dialogue between characters from two different stories. Paired work. | 19 |
| **Writing a script** | To use some of the devices commonly featured in playscripts. To read and understand dialogue within a narrative. | 1c; 2b; 3a. *Imaginative writing: Level E* | Y5 T1 | Producing scripts based on a narrative that contains dialogue. Paired work. | 20 |
| **Turning a drama script into prose, page 93** | | | | | |
| **Snow** | To write imaginatively making use of adverbs and adjectives. | 1b, c; 3b. *Imaginative writing: Level D.* | Y4 T2 | Descriptive writing about snow after going out into the snow and listening to poems which have a snow theme. Individuals. | 22 |
| **Adjective, noun, verb poems, page 41** | | | | | |
| **My best friend** | To write coherently using adverbs and adjectives to enhance their writing. | 3b. *Personal writing: Level D.* | Y4 T1 | Writing about friendship and describing a friend. Individual work. | 23 |

| ACTIVITY TITLE | LEARNING OBJECTIVE | POS/AO | NLS | CONTENT | PAGE |
|---|---|---|---|---|---|
| **Another planet** | To plan and write imaginative extended stories. | 1a, c. *Imaginative writing: Level D.* | Y4 T3 | Writing science fiction stories about a visit to another planet. Individuals. | 24 |
| **Another world, page 32** | | | | | |
| **Bill's new frock** | To write imaginatively in role. | 1a, c. *As above.* | Y6 T1 | Making notes and then writing a story with two different narrators in role, after reading part of Anne Fine's story. Paired work. | 26 |
| **If I were a…, page 38** | | | | | |
| **Flannan Isle** | To write imaginatively in response to a stimulus. To appreciate the use of unusual words in writing from the past. | 1c; 2a. *As above.* | Y5 T2 | Story writing which explains the fate of the missing lighthouse keepers in Gibson's poem. Individual work following a class reading of the poem. | 27 |
| **The fib** | To write a story in the first person, using an episodic structure. | 1b; 2a. *Personal writing: Level C.* | Y3 T3 | Writing a story about a fib after reading George Layton's story. Individual work. | 29 |
| **Changing places** | To write an imaginative story, possibly with two different narrators. | 1c; 2a, b. *Imaginative writing: Level D.* | Y6 T1 | Writing a story about changing lives with someone else. Individuals or pairs. | 30 |
| **A million pounds, page 39** | | | | | |
| **Five-word stories** | To build a story around five key words. To be able to arrive at the best uses of words for different purposes. | 1c; 2a, b. *Imaginative writing: Level C.* | Y4 T2 | Writing stories which must include five key words. Individual work. | 31 |
| **Writing from notes, page 17** | | | | | |
| **Cartoons with captions** | To write suitable captions for cartoon pictures. | 1b; 2a. *As above.* | Y4 T1 | Writing captions for cartoons. Individuals and pairs/groups. | 32 |
| **Group writing using pictures, page 28** | | | | | |
| **Headlines** | To make use of the contents of newspaper reports to write eye-catching headlines. | 1b; 3c. *Functional writing: Level D.* | Y5 T1 | Reading articles and devising appropriate headlines. Individual and group work. | 33 |
| **Writing a report, page 18** | | | | | |
| **Jessica's other house** | To plan, draft, revise, proofread and present an imaginative story based upon the theme of a parallel world. | 1c, b. *Imaginative writing: Level D.* | Y5 T1 | Writing a story based upon travel into a parallel world. Class reading of extracts followed by individual story writing. | 34 |
| **Another world, page 32; A planned story, page 26** | | | | | |
| **Cinquains** | To write a poem in a given format and to understand what a syllable is. | 1c; 2d. *As above.* | Y4 T3 | Writing poems which follow a set formula (five lines of 2, 4, 6, 8 and 2 syllables respectively). Individuals or pairs. | 36 |
| **Haiku, page 46** | | | | | |

| ACTIVITY TITLE | LEARNING OBJECTIVE | POS/AO | NLS | CONTENT | PAGE |
|---|---|---|---|---|---|
| Triolets | To write a poem in a given format and to understand that repetition can be a useful device in poetry. To use rhymes correctly. | 1b; 2a. *As above.* | Y3 T2 | Writing eight-line poems in which the first line reappears as the fourth and seventh and the second reappears as the eighth. Individuals or pairs. | 37 |
| **November, page 47; If…, page 48** | | | | | |
| Character sketches | To write character sketches. | 1b; 2a. *Imaginative writing: Level C.* | Y4 T1 | Writing short descriptions of people which may be negative or positive. Individuals or pairs. | 39 |
| **An interview with a celebrity, page 24** | | | | | |
| Alternative endings | To write an alternative ending for a story. | 1b; 2a. *As above.* | Y4 T3 | Writing alternative endings for familiar stories. Individuals or pairs. | 41 |
| **What happened next? page 30** | | | | | |

**NON-FICTION WRITING**

| ACTIVITY TITLE | LEARNING OBJECTIVE | POS/AO | NLS | CONTENT | PAGE |
|---|---|---|---|---|---|
| Who's who | To write in a style appropriate for a reference book. | 1c; 2a. *Functional writing: Level C.* | Y6 T1 | Writing entries for a class edition of 'Who's Who'. Individuals and then groups. | 42 |
| Making textbooks | To understand the structure of a textbook. | 1b, c. *Functional writing: Level D.* | Y5 T2 | Making use of the children's growing knowledge of the structure of textbooks to allow them to produce their own on a given subject. Children working individually and in small groups. | 43 |
| **Book covers, page 52** | | | | | |
| Passports | To produce a mock version of an official document which includes personal details. | 1b; 2a. *As above.* | Y3 T1 | Making passports based upon real ones and creating databases. Individual work. | 44 |
| Certificates | To use the features of layout and presentation appropriate for certificates. | 1c; 2e. *Functional writing: Level C.* | Y4 T3 | Making certificates for a class awards ceremony. Individuals or pairs. | 45 |
| House specifications | To write persuasively in a style appropriate for a specific purpose. To convey information. | 1c; 2a. *As above.* | Y6 T3 | Reading estate agents' details, then creating brochures which advertise houses and make them attractive to potential buyers. Individual work. | 46 |
| **A guide to the school, page 101** | | | | | |
| A written argument | To write persuasively in a real context. | 1c. *As above.* | Y6 T2 | Writing with a partner who takes an opposing viewpoint on an issue. Paired work, involving turn-taking. | 47 |
| Interpreting charts | To write simple non-chronological reports from known information. | 1b. *Functional writing: Level C.* | Y3 T1 | Explaining in writing the data presented in a table or chart. Pairs or individuals. | 48 |
| **Flow charts, page 59** | | | | | |
| Match reports (1) | To use the characteristics of report writing. | 1c. *Functional writing: Level D.* | Y6 T1 | Writing a report on a sports match after reading examples of match reports. Individuals or pairs. | 50 |

| ACTIVITY TITLE | LEARNING OBJECTIVE | POS/AO | NLS | CONTENT | PAGE |
|---|---|---|---|---|---|
| **Match reports (2)** | To use the characteristics of report writing. | 1c. *As above.* | Y6 T1 | Writing a report on a sports match after watching video highlights. Individuals or pairs. | 51 |
| **Excuse notes** | To write an explanation. To parody a persuasive statement. | 1c. *Functional writing: Level C.* | Y3 T3 or Y5 T2 | Devising humorous absence excuses and writing letters of explanation. Individuals or pairs. | 52 |
| **Mottoes** | To understand the nature of mottoes and to devise their own. | 1b; 2a. *As above.* | | Studying mottoes, then creating mottoes for different organizations. Paired work. | 53 |
| **A class quiz** | To understand how to phrase and punctuate questions. | 2a, c. *As above.* | Y3 T1 | Writing questions for a class book quiz. Paired work. | 54 |
| **Did you know that? page 51** | | | | | |
| **Letter to a councillor** | To write a formal, persuasive letter. | 1c. *As above.* | Y5 T3 | Writing to a local representative about an issue of concern, using the features of a formal letter. Individuals. | 55 |
| **Letters to the editor, page 110** | | | | | |
| **Book advertisements** | To write persuasively using features of presentation appropriate for advertisements. | 1c; 2a, e. *As above.* | Y4 T3 | Preparing and producing an advertisement designed to persuade people to read a particular book. Individuals or pairs. | 56 |
| **Classified ads, page 109** | | | | | |
| **The town (1)** | To write short autobiographies in role. | 1c; 2a. *Personal writing: Level D.* | Y6 T1 | Writing autobiographies of invented characters who live in an imaginary town. Individuals. | 57 |
| **The town (2)** | To write a letter in role. | 1c; 2a. *Functional writing: Level D.* | Y6 T1 | Writing letters in role. Individuals, pairs and groups. | 59 |
| **The town (3)** | To use sequential text to write directions. | 2a. *As above.* | Y6 T1 | Writing sequential directions for journeys within an invented town. Individuals, pairs and groups. | 60 |
| **The town (4)** | To use a journalistic style. | 1c, 2a. *As above.* | Y6 T1 | Writing a newspaper article about an invented town. Individuals, pairs and groups. | 61 |

| ACTIVITY TITLE | LEARNING OBJECTIVE | POS/AO | NLS | CONTENT | PAGE |
|---|---|---|---|---|---|
| **Vocabulary extension (1)** | To identify adverbs and insert them in a passage of prose. | 2a; 3b. *Knowledge about language: Level D.* | Y4 T1 | Making use of a selection of adverbs to enliven a piece of prose. Paired work. | 62 |
| **Vocabulary extension (2)** | To identify adjectives and insert them in a passage of prose. | 2a; 3b. *As above.* | Y3 T2 | Identifying adjectives and replacing them to enliven a piece of prose. Paired work. | 64 |
| **Use of adjectives, page 88** | | | | | |
| **Plurals (1)** | To understand the concept of pluralization and to develop a greater knowledge of regular and irregular noun plurals. | 2d; 3b. *As above.* | Y3 T2 | Matching singulars to plurals, then changing singular nouns to plural nouns in sentences. Individual or paired work. | 65 |
| **Plurals (2)** | To understand the concept of pluralization and to develop a greater knowledge of regular and irregular noun plurals. | 2d; 3b. *As above.* | Y3 T2 | Changing singulars to plurals in a piece of text. Individual or paired work. | 67 |
| **Subordinate clauses and phrases** | To understand the value of subordinate clauses and phrases and to be able to make use of them in writing. | 3b. *As above.* | Y6; T1/2/3 | Incorporating subordinate clauses and phrases into text. Individuals or pairs. | 68 |
| **Clauses and phrases, page 85** | | | | | |
| **Past tense** | To understand the concept of the past tense and the present tense. | 2a; 3b. *As above.* | Y4 T3 | Rewriting a passage from the present tense into the past tense. Individuals or pairs. | 70 |
| **Verb exchange** | To identify verbs and replace them with alternative verbs. | 3b. *As above.* | Y3 T1 | Replacing all the verbs in sentences with alternative ones. Paired work. | 71 |
| **Proofreading** | To make use of prompts to revise and edit a piece of prose. | 2b. *Punctuation and structure: Level D; Spelling: Level D.* | Y3 T2 | Using a list to check, correct, revise and edit a prepared piece of text. Individuals or pairs. | 73 |
| **Confusing sentences** | To understand how clauses and phrases can be manipulated to achieve different effects. | 2c. *Knowledge about language: Level D.* | Y5 T2 Y6 T1/3 | Looking at examples of confusing sentences and rewriting them. Paired work. | 74 |
| **Simple English** | To understand the importance of choosing appropriate vocabulary for a younger audience and to make use of reference sources. | 2a; 3a. *Functional writing: Level D.* | Y5 T2 | Simplifying text so that it is more concise. Paired work. | 76 |
| **Nursery stories for younger children, page 36** | | | | | |
| **Presentation** | To use a style of handwriting appropriate for presenting an attractive piece of work. | 2e. *Handwriting and presentation: Level D.* | Y4 T1/2 | Writing out a poem, presenting it with an awareness of presentational devices. Individuals. | 77 |

LANGUAGE STUDY

| ACTIVITY TITLE | LEARNING OBJECTIVE | POS/AO | NLS | CONTENT | PAGE |
|---|---|---|---|---|---|
| Apostrophes | To understand the correct usage of apostrophes for elision and possession. | 2d. *Knowledge about language: Level E.* | Y4 T2 Y5 T3 | Correcting examples of incorrect usage of apostrophes in a piece of prose. Individuals. | 78 |
| **Apostrophes for abbreviation, page 83; Apostrophes for possession, page 84** | | | | | |
| Changing sentences | To understand how the grammar of a sentence alters when the sentence type is changed. | 2d. *Knowledge about lanaguage: Level D.* | Y4 T3 | Working on photocopiable texts to convert sentences into questions and negative statements. Pairs. | 80 |
| **Unfinished sentences, page 69; Question marks, page 70** | | | | | |
| Arranging sentences | To understand the importance of sentence order in establishing the meaning of a text. | 3b. *Punctuation and structure: Level D.* | Y4 T2 | Taking jumbled sentences and rearranging them into a logical order before sorting them into paragraphs. Individuals or pairs. | 81 |
| **Combining sentences, page 68** | | | | | |
| Organizing notes | To use notes to draft writing. | 2b. *Functional writing: Level D.* | Y5 T1 | Using prepared rough notes to write prose using headings and subheadings. | 82 |
| Varying expression | To reflect upon language use and to consider ways of varying expression. | 3a, c. *Knowledge about language: Level D.* | Y5 T2 Y6 | Taking sentences and rewriting them in different ways, while retaining original meanings. Individuals or pairs. | 84 |
| Comparative adjectives | To understand the different ways in which comparative and superlative adjectives may be written. | 3b, c. *As above.* | Y4 T2 | Selecting the appropriate comparative or superlative adjective for sentences. Individuals or pairs. | 85 |
| **Use of adjectives, page 88** | | | | | |
| Speech marks | To convert text from reported speech to direct speech. | 2c. *Punctuation and structure: Level D.* | Y5 T1 | Changing reported speech into direct speech by using speech marks. Individuals or pairs working from photocopiables and then independently. | 86 |

# Imaginative writing

In this chapter a range of activities is provided which should provide stimuli to enable children to write imaginatively in prose and poetic forms.

If they are to write well, children will need to be introduced to a variety of published texts and should have regular experience of hearing stories and poems read aloud to them. Opportunities should be sought to discuss vocabulary and phrasing and they should be encouraged to draw upon this rich store of language when writing themselves.

Most of the activities include suggestions for adaptation for Literacy Hour work. While it is important that children have lots of opportunities for extended writing, not least because this is demanded in National tests, it is also vital that they are given the chance to look at text closely. The Literacy Hour provides the occasion for this and can, if well-managed, lead naturally into extended writing. Typically, the Literacy Hour might be used to discuss text and to prepare children's introductions or plans for extended writing in a subsequent lesson.

Throughout the activities, terms are used which feature in the glossary for the National Literacy Strategy *Framework for Teaching*. Most children can understand these easily when they are explained within the context of their own and other people's writing. An understanding of this terminology should enable children to discuss their writing and to share ideas with others.

It is hoped that in their work in imaginative writing children will both extend their knowledge of their own language and enjoy exploring its usage.

## THE BROKEN WINDOW

*To write additional text in the style of an author, after attempting to use the style to create a story opening.*

†† *Whole-class work followed by individual or group work.*

⏰ *At least one hour.*

### Previous skills/knowledge needed
The children will need to understand what is meant by an author's style. In advance of the lesson, you could look for interesting story openings and read some to the class.

### Key background information
In this activity children are introduced to a story opening which creates tension. They are then asked to write their own story openings in a style similar to that of the author. The lesson should provide the prelude to further extended writing as children continue the stories and attempt to resolve issues within them.

*Literacy Hour:* this activity could form part of a series of Literacy Hours which focus on writing in the style of an author. It may be used in Y5 or Y6 but might be particularly suitable for Y5 in Term 3 (T9).

### Preparation
Make an enlarged copy of photocopiable pages 88 and 89, or make multiple copies so that children can share the story in pairs. Find other examples of children being in trouble and have them available so that children can refer to them in the activity, if they wish. *Danny the Champion of the World* by Roald Dahl (Puffin) has a passage in which Danny is wrongly accused and punished for cheating, which you may find suitable.

### Resources needed
Photocopiable pages 88 and 89, other examples of similar texts, board or flip chart, paper, writing materials.

### What to do
*Introduction*
Read the story with the children and discuss the content. Ask the children how they would have felt in Jessica's position and invite them to describe occasions when they have been in trouble. Do not push children to contribute memories if they do not wish to. Write on the board any significant words and phrases which the children suggest and ask them to look for words and phrases in the story which show how Jessica felt. Discuss the style of the passage and talk about the way in which the author creates

tension. Explain the idea of suspense – a tension about what is going to happen next. In the first four paragraphs they might look at the following clauses and phrases:

*every breath was held as the ball sped towards the staffroom window, then there was a shattering, crashing sound as the glass exploded into a thousand pieces;*
*the playground fell silent and there was an awful hush before a loud, shrill adult voice broke the silence;*
*Miss Carmichael's red and angry face appeared at the smashed staffroom window and her eyes scanned the playground;*
*in a voice which trembled with fear.*

Ask them to think about a story which they would like to write and to consider similar phrases which might excite the reader.

*Individual/group work*

Ask the children to write four short opening paragraphs similar to those in the passage, which create tension and introduce a story in which someone appears to be in trouble. They should follow the style of the author of the Jessica story and should look for opportunities to grab the reader's attention.

Explain that they will be able to continue their openings and write at greater length later, but that the focus for the lesson is the creation of a tension which will make the reader want to know what happens next.

## Suggestion(s) for extension

When children are happy with their opening passages, ask them to write the next section of their stories. You may wish to confine them to writing a single section or you may want to let them complete the stories.

## Suggestion(s) for support

Some children could work in pairs or with an adult scribe who could help them to write their openings. You may wish to work on shared or guided writing with a group of children to help them to produce a piece of writing which they could then continue independently or in pairs. (Also, see 'Opportunities for IT' below.)

## Assessment opportunities

Look for evidence that children are able to use devices such as short sentences, adjectives and adverbs to create tension. Note their ability to write in a style which is similar to that in the story.

## Opportunities for IT

Ask some children to use the word processor to write and edit their stories. For children with limited writing skills, you may wish to key in the opening four paragraphs of the story and make back-up copies of the file before allowing the children to edit and change them to create their own pieces of writing.

## Display ideas

Display an enlarged version of the opening four paragraphs of 'The broken window: part one' together with copies of the children's opening four paragraphs.

## Other aspects of the English PoS covered

Reading – 1d, 2b.
Speaking and listening – 1a.

## Reference to photocopiable sheets

Photocopiable pages 88 and 89 show the opening pages of a story in which various literary techniques are used to create a sense of fear and suspense. The children can use this as a stimulus for their own writing.

### The broken window: part one

There was a horrible moment when every breath was held as the ball sped towards the staffroom window, then there was a shattering, crashing sound as the glass exploded into a thousand pieces.

The players stopped. Everyone in the playground fell silent and there was an awful hush before a loud, stern adult voice broke the silence. "Who on earth is responsible for this?"

Miss Carmichael's red and angry face appeared at the smashed staffroom window and her eyes scanned the playground. "Come along, I want to know who broke this window immediately, if not sooner!"

The playground remained silent and still for a few seconds longer and then Jessica stepped forward and raised her hand. "I'm sorry Miss, it was me," she said in a voice which trembled with fear.

"You, Jessica Scott, you? You kicked a ball so hard that it smashed the staffroom window? Go and stand outside my office and wait for me there!"

As Jessica trudged from the playground, the other children stood silently watching her. She was near to tears as she feared the punishment that Miss Carmichael might give to her. She had read stories in which children at private schools were given hundreds of lines to write or were made to pick up litter for a week. She had even read of children being beaten. As she trooped across the playground, she thought of running away and going back to the house at Little Row... she would wait until dark before... through the trapdoor... this place.

Her t... the sou... and th... eyes s...

### The broken window: part one (cont.)

then all together, the other children were applauding her. "Great shot, Scotty!" called Kenneth, and the others joined in with similar cries. Amanda ran to her and put an arm around her shoulders. "Don't worry, Jessica," she said, "it won't be all that bad."

Jessica didn't know whether to be happy about the reaction of the others or terrified about the action that Miss Carmichael might take. The headteacher had been friendly when she had called her into her office the day before, but now she sounded angry and fierce. Jessica climbed the stairs to the office as slowly as if she were about to have a tooth out at the dentist's. There was no chair outside Miss Carmichael's room, so she stood uncomfortably, hopping from foot to foot, thinking about the dreadful punishment that she might be given.

After what seemed an hour, but what was probably only about five minutes, Miss Carmichael's footsteps could be heard coming up the stairs getting louder and more menacing as they neared her office. Jessica hardly dared to look at her as she reached the end of the corridor. "Well may you avoid my eyes, young lady!" thundered Miss Carmichael in a voice which confirmed Jessica's worst fears. "Go into my office!"

Jessica could hardly turn the doorknob, her hands were shaking so much. After a few moments of fumbling she managed to open the door and entered the room followed by the headteacher.

# GIRLS DON'T PLAY FOOTBALL

*To write persuasively.*

†† *Individuals, pairs and groups.*

🕑 *One and a half hours.*

## Previous skills/knowledge needed

This activity uses the second part of 'The broken window' story and should only be attempted after the first part has been read.

## Key background information

The passage takes place in a headteacher's study after Jessica has broken a window playing football. Miss Carmichael surprises Jessica by praising her for playing football and by saying that it is quite acceptable for girls as well as boys to play the game. However, she makes some provocative statements first and Jessica defends women's football.

*Literacy Hour:* this lesson could form part of a series of Literacy Hours for Y5 T3 (T19) which focus on constructing and presenting arguments.

## Preparation

Make multiple copies of photocopiable pages 90 and 91, and/or an enlargement, which can be read with the children. Ann Fine's *Bill's New Frock* (Mammoth) has an excellent passage in which Bill, who has become a girl for the day, discovers that girls are left with virtually nowhere to play because the playground is dominated by boys playing football. This passage could be read to the children in preparation for this activity.

## Resources needed

Photocopiable pages 90 and 91, board or flip chart, paper, writing materials.

## What to do

*Introduction*

Remind the children about what happened in part one of the story and ask them to talk about the way Jessica might be feeling as she waits to see Miss Carmichael.

Read the passage to them and ask them to comment especially about how they think Jessica's emotions might have changed during her interview with the headteacher. Explain that you want them to think about the conversation about girls playing football and ask for their opinions. Write

*for* and *against* on the board and make a note of the children's views under each heading.

Be prepared for some boys to say things like 'Girls aren't good enough' or 'They're not strong enough'. There are, as Jessica points out, professional teams for women in Italy, and women play a high standard of football in national leagues in Britain. However, Football Association rules do not allow post-primary aged boys and girls to play in the same teams. This could be a matter which the children could debate. As to girls' strength, you will probably find that many of the girls in your class are bigger than the boys and you could easily demonstrate this!

*Individual/group work*

Ask the children to work independently or in pairs to make notes on their arguments for and against girls playing football or, if they prefer, boys playing netball. After a few minutes, bring the class together (the debate is usually lively and noisy!) and ask some children to present their views to the class.

Show the children how to write an opening paragraph for a piece of persuasive writing by taking one of their viewpoints and introducing it. Ask the children to return to their writing and to turn their notes into a piece of persuasive writing.

## Suggestion(s) for extension

You may wish to develop this lesson into a series of lessons which include an oral debate. Some children could find out more about women's football and about the Football Association's ruling. They may even wish to write to the FA to express their views.

## Suggestion(s) for support

Some children could confine their writing to making a 'for' and 'against' chart which could be created in pairs by children with opposing views.

## Assessment opportunities

Look for evidence that children are able to write persuasively and that they can articulate their ideas and present them rationally.

## Opportunities for IT

Children could look for information on women's football through the Internet if it is available in the school.

## Display ideas

Display 'The broken window, part two' together with the children's persuasive writing. You may wish to add a 'for' and 'against' chart with short passages written by children pinned in the appropriate columns. The children could add more ideas as they think of new arguments after the lesson.

## Other aspects of the English PoS covered

Reading – 2b.
Speaking and listening – 2b.

## Reference to photocopiable sheets

Photocopiable pages 90 and 91 provide a continuation of the story which was begun on page 88. The children can use it as a stimulus to explore opposed arguments and to attempt their own persuasive writing.

## THE LION POEMS

*To use experience of published texts to help structure their own writing. To appreciate that different graphemes can represent the same phoneme.*

†† *Whole-class work followed by individual and group work.*

🕐 *At least one hour.*

### Previous skills/knowledge needed

Children will need to have read the two poems and should be aware of different ways in which rhyming patterns can be set out.

### Key background information

In this activity the children listen to and read two well-known poems which tell stories of children being eaten by lions. They are then asked to write their own stories or poems on a similar theme. The poems are both light-hearted and neither is particularly gruesome.

*Literacy Hour:* this lesson could begin as a Literacy Hour and lead in to extended writing or it could form part of a series of Literacy Hours for Y6 (especially in Term 2) in which children parody a variety of literary texts. Alternatively, the lessons could be devised for Y5 T2 (T11), with children using the themes of the poems to write their own versions.

### Preparation

Find copies of *The Lion and Albert* by Marriott Edgar which appears in Stanley Holloway's *Monologues* (Elm Tree Books) and *Jim* by Hilaire Belloc which appears in *Cautionary Verses* (Red Fox). If allowed by your school's photocopying licence, provide multiple copies of each poem.

### Resources needed

*The Lion and Albert* by Marriott Edgar and *Jim* by Hilaire Belloc, board or flip chart, writing materials.

### What to do

*Introduction*

Begin by reading one of the poems, with the children following and/or reading it with you. Discuss with them the key events in the poem and ask them to think about the ways in which the poet uses language to affect the reader's emotions. Discuss the use of verbs, adverbs and adjectives and make a note on the board of those which the children find particularly significant.

*Individual/group work*

Ask the children to make notes on the key events in the poem and then write the story briefly.

Now read the other poem to the children and discuss it

in the same way. This time draw attention to similarities and differences between the poems. The children could have pieces of paper divided down the middle on which they could note similarities on one side and differences on the other.

Explain that the children are going to write their own story poem on a similar theme to the two poems and that they should choose the style of one to write in. Discuss the rhyme structures with them. (They may work best in pairs for this activity.) Inevitably, they may struggle to find rhymes, but this can be a source of humour for the poems; tell them that in a humorous poem it is acceptable to have strange rhymes because they can sometimes make the reader laugh. Help them to find rhyming words, then discuss them and note the words on the board.

## Suggestion(s) for extension
This activity could be repeated for some children, using more serious poems or stories.

## Suggestion(s) for support
Provide some children with lists of pairs of rhyming words that are appropriate to the story and ask them to build their poems around them.

## Assessment opportunities
Look for signs that children are able to appreciate that different clusters of letters may produce the same sound. For example, do they appreciate that although *fun* and *son*, and *through* and *zoo* rhyme, they have different graphemes to represent a similar sound? Look for evidence that the children are able to adopt the style of the poets in their own writing.

## Opportunities for IT
Ask some children to compose their poems on the word processor and encourage them to use the editing facilities to develop and refine their work. They can then devise a suitable layout for their completed poems using the tab key or centre command.

## Display ideas
Display copies of Belloc's and Edgar's poems surrounded by the children's work. Add pictures of lions taken from books and magazines, as well as some that have been drawn or painted by the children.

## Other aspects of the English PoS covered
Reading – 1d.
Speaking and listening – 2a.

# DEAR JACK

*To write an explanation in role for an audience. To write an informal letter.*
†† *Whole-class work followed by individual work.*
⊕ *At least one hour.*

## Previous skills/knowledge needed
Children will need to know the story of Jack and the Beanstalk and understand how letters are set out.

## Key background information
This activity is intended to encourage children to explore characterization. It involves discussing a well-known story with the children and looking at the characteristics of two characters before writing letters in role.

*Literacy Hour:* this lesson could form part of a series of Literacy Hours for Y5 T3 (T7) in which children write in role. It could also be used in Y4 T1.

## Preparation
Make an enlarged copy of photocopiable page 92. Find a copy of the story of Jack and the Beanstalk.

## Resources needed
Photocopiable page 92, the story *Jack and the Beanstalk*, board or flip chart, paper, writing materials.

## What to do
*Introduction*
Discuss the two main characters from the story of Jack and the Beanstalk: Jack and the Giant. Ask the children to help you to write a brief character sketch of one of them. Model the use of adjectives to describe the character and show how careful selection of words is important in determining how the character appears to the reader. As an alternative, you may wish to use characters from a story which is currently being read to the children.

*Individual/group work*
Read the example of a letter on photocopiable page 92 and ask the children whether they think the Giant is a good or a bad person. Do they believe what he says? The letter is written in an informal style and this should be discussed briefly with the children as should other features of such letters – the position of the sender's address, the date, the way in which the letter begins and the way in which it ends.

Explain to the children that they are going to write a letter from Jack in response to the Giant's letter. Tell them that they will need to refer to events from the story and that they should write from the point of view of the character. The writing should therefore be in the first person and should include an explanation for Jack's actions. Before they begin, ask the children to make notes on the character of Jack and on the things he did in the story.

## Suggestion(s) for extension

Give the children the task of writing letters from the Giant to Jack which respond to Jack's letters. Swap the letters around so that the children respond to someone else writing in role. This could lead to a whole series of letters being written.

## Suggestion(s) for support

Some children could write the letters with the help of a partner or an adult scribe. You may wish to work with one group to create a wordbank of useful words (for example, *dear, yours, sincerely, faithfully* and other words that might figure in this particular letter) and then let the children use them as a framework for their writing. If the words are written on card or on slips of paper, children can arrange them in a suitable order and then write sentences which include them.

### Dear Jack...

The Castle
Stalk Top
FEF1 F0

Dear Jack                                              21 October

As you probably know, I have been very tired lately. It is hard work looking after the whole castle and my wife is not as young as she used to be.

I have been trying to save the golden eggs the goose lays, so that I can sell them and be able to afford to pay someone to come and cook and clean for us. Unfortunately, every time I come down the beanstalk and go to the bank, everyone runs away screaming. Another problem is that I am too big to get through the door of the bank!

I expect you were pretty frightened the other day when I woke up and chased you and I don't blame you for chopping the beanstalk down. The castle was quite badly damaged, so my wife and I have decided to move to another area and set up home there.

Anyway, I'm sorry I was so cross and I honestly would never have hurt you, but I wonder if you would do me a great favour. You see, we need some money to build a house and now that you have taken our golden goose, we just don't have any. Do you think you could lend me the goose for a few days so that it could lay some golden eggs for us? I would give the goose back to you as soon as I had finished, honestly. There is a bank near here where I think they would exchange the eggs for cash. I went the other day and the manager said he would do anything for me as long as I didn't hurt him.

Please write back and tell me that you will help us. It will soon be winter and I really feel the cold.

Best wishes

Giant

## Assessment opportunities

Look for evidence that children are able to adopt the conventions of informal letter writing, and look for signs that they are able to draw upon the characteristics of Jack and the Giant when writing in role.

## Opportunities for IT

Try writing key words and phrases in a file and then asking the children to use them as starting points for their own writing. Remember to make back-up copies of the file so that it may be reused.

## Display ideas

Display letters from Jack on one side of a large painting of a beanstalk with a castle at the top, and display letters from the Giant on the other. Write a number in the corner of the letters from Jack and a letter in the corner of those from the Giant. When children have finished some work, you could ask them to read the letters and match the letters and numbers, finding a different response for each letter.

## Other aspects of the English PoS covered

Reading – 2b.
Speaking and listening – 1c.

## Reference to photocopiable sheet

Photocopiable page 92 shows a letter from the Giant to Jack which gives an imaginary 'sequel' to the familiar story. It combines aspects of explanation and persuasion. The children can use it as a model for their own imaginative letters.

# IMAGINARY DIALOGUE

**To use speech marks accurately in imaginative writing.**

†† *Whole-class work followed by paired work.*

⊕ *At least one hour.*

## Previous skills/knowledge needed

Children will need to understand how dialogue is set out and should be aware that it is now equally acceptable to use single or double inverted commas providing the writer is consistent.

They will need to be familiar with the characters of Cinderella and Goldilocks as well as the outlines of the traditional stories in which they feature.

The lesson may be used as a follow-up to the previous activity, 'Dear Jack', although this is not essential.

## Key background information

This activity is intended to develop and reinforce the use of speech marks and the writing of dialogue through imaginative writing. It is followed up by the activity 'Writing a script' and is also linked to 'Speech marks' (see page 86).

*Literacy Hour:* this lesson could be part of Literacy Hour work for Y5 T1 (S7 and T15).

## Preparation

Make an enlarged version of photocopiable page 93. Find examples of dialogue from books in the classroom.

## Resources needed

Photocopiable page 93, paper, writing materials. A selection of books which the children have read or had read to them, for extension activity.

## What to do

*Introduction*

Show the children an enlarged version of the conversation between Goldilocks and Cinderella. Explain that the two never appeared in the same story, but that the author has tried to imagine what it might be like if they met and talked to each other.

Read the conversation with them and then give two children the parts of the characters and ask them to read the lines that are actually spoken (they should miss out

the rest of the text, which will be left to you and the rest of the class to speak). The dialogue includes an example of speech within speech when Cinderella tells Goldilocks what the fairy godmother said. Use this as an opportunity to discuss the way in which such speech can be punctuated by using single inverted commas if double inverted commas have already been used, or vice versa.

*Individual/group work*

This work may take place over a series of lessons (after you have used an introductory session each time to discuss the accurate use of speech marks). In the first lesson, ask all children to work in pairs to continue the dialogue between Goldilocks and Cinderella. Ask one child in each pair to write as Goldilocks and the other as Cinderella, writing on a shared sheet of paper. Encourage one child to make notes on a separate sheet of paper to prepare the next speech while the other child is writing on the shared sheet of paper.

In subsequent lessons, ask the children to write dialogues between characters from other stories. Encourage them to make use of humour. Explain that within speech it is acceptable to use abbreviated forms of words such as *don't, can't* and *wouldn't*, which would not normally be used in texts. They may also wish to use slang and colloquialisms which are acceptable in speech.

## Suggestion(s) for extension

Ask the children to look through books for examples of dialogue and ask them to find different words which authors use to show how characters speak, for example *said, cried, shouted, replied, whispered* and *exclaimed*. They could make a list for display and this could be added to as other words are discovered in future reading, the list being used as a resource by the whole class.

## Suggestion(s) for support

Some children could be given one of the character's side of a conversation and then be asked to write the other person's words. They may require help to formulate their own writing and this could be provided by you or by an adult helper. Alternatively, you could provide the text on a computer file and provide some words which will help the children to write the missing dialogue so that they can build sentences around them.

## Assessment opportunities

Look for evidence that children are able to use speech marks and associated punctuation accurately. Look for evidence of lively and interesting writing of dialogue.

## Opportunities for IT

See 'Suggestion(s) for support'.

## Display ideas

Display the children's dialogues together with examples from well-known books with which the children are familiar. The display could become a focus for future work in which children are asked to write the next two speeches for each dialogue.

### Goldilocks and Cinderella in conversation (1)

"So go on, tell me about this fairy godmother of yours," said Goldilocks.
"Well, it was strange really," said Cinderella. "One minute I was scrubbing the kitchen floor and keeping an eye on a pan full of porridge, and the next I was looking at this peculiar old lady who was wearing a silver dress and carrying a magic wand."
"Porridge, eh?" said Goldilocks. "I'm rather fond of porridge."
"Look, do you want to hear my story or not?" asked Cinderella huffily.
"Of course I do," replied Goldilocks. "I'm sorry, but I had rather a nasty experience the other day."
"Well tell me about it later. It's my turn now!" said Cinderella crossly. "Now where was I?"
"You had just met a lady in a silver dress who carried a magic wand," prompted Goldilocks.
"Ah yes. Well she just looked at me kneeling on the floor surrounded by soap suds and she smelled the porridge on the stove and she asked me if I needed a night out."
"And what did you say?"
"I told her that would be wonderful and I asked her if she was going to scrub the floor and make the porridge while I went to a disco. 'Oh no,' she said, 'I don't scrub floors. I do magic!'"
"What happened?" asked Goldilocks eagerly.
"Well she just sort of waved her wand and suddenly I was wearing a beautiful dress and the floor was clean and the porridge had disappeared. Then she told me to go to the window and, as I did, she waved her wand again and turned mice and pumpkins into a coach and horses. I don't mind telling you, I was speechless."
"That would make a change!" laughed Goldilocks.
"Look, if you're going to be cheeky, I'm not going to tell you any more," grumbled Cinderella.
"I'm sorry," said Goldilocks, "please carry on."

## Other aspects of the English PoS covered

Reading – 1c.
Speaking and listening – 1b.

## Reference to photocopiable sheet

Photocopiable page 93 shows a possible dialogue between Goldilocks and Cinderella. This can be used as a stimulus for work on the writing and punctuation of direct speech in a narrative.

---

## WRITING A SCRIPT

*To use some of the devices commonly featured in playscripts. To read and understand dialogue within a narrative.*

†† *Whole-class work followed by paired work.*

🕐 *At least one hour.*

### Previous skills/knowledge needed

Children will need to be aware of the ways in which scripts are set out, and it will be helpful if they have completed the previous activity 'Imaginary dialogue'.

### Key background information

This activity is intended to develop children's familiarity with the format of a script. Ideally, it could be done before children begin to prepare for a school performance in which scripts need to be read and lines learned. The activity could be linked to other work on dialogue in 'Speech marks' (see page 86).

*Literacy Hour:* this lesson could be part of Literacy Hour work for Y5 T1 (S7) or Y4 T1 (T13).

### Preparation

Find examples of playscripts which are within the children's reading capabilities. The scripted versions of some of Roald Dahl's stories may be ideal. Show these to the children so that they can see the layout of a playscript.

Have to hand the enlarged copy of photocopiable page 93 featuring Goldilocks and Cinderella in Conversation used in the previous activity 'Imaginary dialogue' and make an enlargement of photocopiable page 94.

### Resources needed

Examples of playscripts (see 'Preparation'), photocopiable pages 93 and 94, writing materials.

### What to do

*Introduction*

Show the children the enlarged photocopiable sheet 'Goldilocks and Cinderella in conversation (1)' which is presented with speech marks and remind them about the way dialogue is set out. Explain that you want to show them how the same spoken words can be set out in script form. Show them just the first two lines of page 94 and ask them to compare these with the dialogue format. Now ask the children to suggest how the next line should be written. Continue to show them the script and the dialogue until you are confident that they understand how dialogue can be presented in script form.

*Individual/group work*

Ask the children to work in pairs to rewrite the dialogue from 'Goldilocks and Cinderella in conversation (1)' into script form. Encourage them to set the script out carefully

and tell them that they may put directions in brackets to show how lines should be spoken.

When they have completed the transformation of the dialogue into script, ask them to write further lines for Goldilocks and Cinderella's conversation.

Finally, look at the script presented on photocopiable page 94 and ask the children to compare the way it is written with their own versions. Check their knowledge of correct layout by asking:

▲ How do you know who is speaking each line?

▲ Why are some words in brackets?

▲ Why are some words in one of Cinderella's speeches set within speech marks?

## Suggestion(s) for extension

Let the children go on to rewrite passages of dialogue from favourite stories into script form. You may feel that some are ready to write their own scripts in preparation for a performance for the class or the school.

## Suggestion(s) for support

Help those children who find it difficult to identify which words in the dialogue are spoken by underlining a few of the pieces of text which are within speech marks. Talk about the way in which inverted commas are used to indicate which words are spoken and to separate these from other parts of the text.

## Assessment opportunities

Look for evidence that children are able to identify speech within text and that they understand the use of speech marks. Note their ability to write in script form and look for an understanding of stage directions.

## Opportunities for IT

The activity lends itself to IT work if the dialogue is keyed in and then the children are able to use the 'cut' and 'paste' facilities to turn it into a script.

## Display ideas

Display some of the children's scripts together with examples of published playscripts. You may wish to create a display which represents a stage by draping curtains at each side and painting a backdrop, then asking some children to paint Goldilocks and Cinderella and other characters from their stories as actors on stage.

## Other aspects of the English PoS covered

Reading – 1c.
Speaking and listening – 1d.

## Reference to photocopiable sheet

Photocopiable page 94 is designed to provide an example for the children of how a dialogue can be written as a script.

### Goldilocks and Cinderella in conversation (2)

GOLDILOCKS: So go on, tell me about this fairy godmother of yours.
CINDERELLA: Well, it was strange really. One minute I was scrubbing the kitchen floor and keeping an eye on a pan full of porridge and the next I was looking at this peculiar old lady who was wearing a silver dress and carrying a magic wand.
GOLDILOCKS: Porridge, eh? I'm rather fond of porridge.
CINDERELLA: Look do you want to hear my story or not?
GOLDILOCKS: Of course I do. I'm sorry, but I had rather a nasty experience the other day.
CINDERELLA: (impatiently) Well tell me about it later. It's my turn now! Now where was I?
GOLDILOCKS: You had just met a lady in a silver dress who carried a magic wand.
CINDERELLA: Ah yes. Well she just looked at me kneeling on the floor surrounded by soap suds and she smelled the porridge on the stove and she asked me if I needed a night out.
GOLDILOCKS: And what did you say?
CINDERELLA: I told her that would be wonderful and I asked her if she was going to scrub the floor and make the porridge while I went to a disco. "Oh no," she said, "I don't scrub floors. I do magic!"
GOLDILOCKS: What happened?
CINDERELLA: Well she just sort of waved her wand and suddenly I was wearing a beautiful dress and the floor was clean and the porridge had disappeared. Then she told me to go to the window and, as I did, she waved her wand again and turned mice and pumpkins into a coach and horses. I don't mind telling you, I was speechless.
GOLDILOCKS: (laughing) That would make a change!
CINDERELLA: (crossly) Look, if you're going to be cheeky, I'm not going to tell you any more.
GOLDILOCKS: I'm sorry, please carry on.

## SNOW

***To write imaginatively making use of adverbs and adjectives.***

†† *Whole-class work followed by individual work.*

🕐 *At least one hour.*

### Key background information

There are many excellent examples of writing about snow. This activity introduces children to some poems and extracts from stories which feature descriptive writing about snow and allows them to write their own descriptions. Clearly, such work is best done when there is snow on the ground and the children can go out and explore it!

*Literacy Hour:* this lesson could form part of a series of Literacy Hours for Y4 T2 which focus on a theme of using expressive language and writing poems based on the structure and/or style of poems read (T13 and T22).

### Preparation

Find a selection of poems about snow. These might include 'Snow' by Leonard Clark from *The Young Puffin Book of Verse* (Penguin); 'Stopping by the Woods on a Snowy Evening' by Robert Frost in *The Faber Book of Children's Verse* (Faber); 'Death of a Snowman' and 'Snow Dream' by Vernon Scannell in *Poets in Hand* (Penguin).

### Resources needed

Poems about snow (see 'Preparation'), board or flip chart, paper, writing materials, snow!

### What to do

*Introduction*

Take the children out into the snow. This is best done immediately after playtime when they are already suitably dressed and have just experienced the snow.

Ask them to think about their feelings about the snow: do they like it? Do they look forward to it snowing? What does the snow look like? How does it change as the weather changes? What games do they play in the snow? What does it feel like?

Don't stay outside for too long and remember that when you come in it will take the children some time to change and to be ready to start work.

Once inside, ask the children to suggest some ideas for describing the snow using the questions you asked when they were outside. Write some key words on the board.

Read some examples of poems about snow and ask the children for their opinions on them.

*Individual/group work*

Explain that you want the children to spend a few minutes jotting down their ideas about snow, and ask them to do this quickly without worrying too much about presentation. Tell them that the notes they make will help them to write in more detail later.

When they have made notes, ask the children to review them and to decide which they wish to use and which they would rather discard. Tell them to use the notes which they like best as a starting point for writing descriptively. They should not, at this stage, attempt to write poetry unless they really want to. The emphasis should be upon using adverbs and adjectives to describe verbs and nouns related to the snow. Encourage the children to revise and edit their work and emphasize that it is better to write a few lines of high quality work than to write pages of work which is not as good.

### Suggestion(s) for extension

Ask the children to turn their writing into poetry using rhyme, but emphasize that it is important that rhymes should not be too contrived.

### Suggestion(s) for support

Make sure that children who may find the activity difficult sit where they can see the key words and phrases which you wrote on the board. Encourage them to draw upon these to help them to produce writing in complete sentences.

### Assessment opportunities

Look for evidence of accurate and imaginative use of adverbs and adjectives which describe verbs and nouns respectively. Where children write rhymes, make a note of any misconceptions about phonemes and be prepared to address these in future lessons.

### Opportunities for IT

Provide a bank of words and phrases related to snow and ask the children to use the 'cut' and 'paste' facilities to move them into a preferred order before writing around them to create their own descriptive passages. Remember to make back-up copies so that the activity can be repeated.

### Display ideas

Display the children's writing together with published examples of poems and prose about snow. The display could incorporate paintings of snow scenes. Ask the children to cut out some snowflake shapes – each snowflake could have an adjective or adverb or a short phrase which each child selects from his or her work – and hang the snowflakes from cotton thread in front of the display to enhance the decorative effect.

### Other aspects of the English PoS covered

Reading – 1d.

Speaking and listening – 1a.

# MY BEST FRIEND

*To write coherently using adverbs and adjectives to enhance their writing.*

†† *Whole-class work followed by individual work.*

⏰ *At least one hour.*

## Previous skills/knowledge needed

Children will need to understand what adverbs and adjectives are and how they can be used to enhance their writing.

## Key background information

This activity allows children to write an affectionate account of their best friend. It should promote the use of adverbs and adjectives and, where appropriate, humour. Problems may be encountered where some children do not appear to have many friends. If you feel that this is the case, you may wish to focus the activity on an ideal rather than an actual friend.

*Literacy Hour:* this lesson could be developed into a series of Literacy Hours for Y4 T1 as follows:
▲ Hour 1: focus on shared reading of descriptions of friendship and vocabulary of friendship (T11)
▲ Hour 2: focus on shared writing, note-making and use of adverbs and adjectives (S4, T11)
▲ Hour 3: focus on turning notes into a character sketch, following further shared reading of model texts (T9).

## Preparation

Find some examples of descriptions of friends which appear in children's stories. For example, Sheila Lavalle's *My Best Fiend* (Puffin), *The Fiend Next Door* (Puffin) and *The Trouble with the Fiend* (Puffin) are affectionate tales of a friendship which is constantly threatened by the bad behaviour of Angela, who regularly gets her friend, Charlie, into trouble. Make copies of photocopiable page 95 as appropriate (see 'What to do').

## Resources needed

Photocopiable page 95, examples of writing about friendship, paper, board or flip chart, writing materials. Thesauruses for extension activity.

## What to do

*Introduction*

Read some extracts from stories which feature friendships and ask the children to suggest how the authors show that people are friends. With the children's help, build up a bank of words associated with friendship, writing the words on the board. These might include:
▲ words for *friend* such as: *pal, buddy, mate, chum, comrade, companion* and *colleague*
▲ adjectives used to describe friends' qualities such as: *loyal, faithful, affectionate, trustworthy* and *sympathetic*
▲ verbs which relate to friendship such as: *welcome, like, love, protect, sympathize* and *befriend*
▲ adverbs which could describe the ways in which friends do things such as: *happily, cheerfully, carefully, thoughtfully, considerately* and *skilfully*.

Discuss with the children the qualities which they would look for in an ideal friend and write some of these on the board.

*Individual/group work*

Ask the children to write in note form about their actual best friend or an ideal best friend. Explain that they are not going to write a story, but are going to write a description of a person who has the particular qualities which they seek in a friend. Provide copies of photocopiable page 95 for those children who need a framework for their preparatory notes.

When the children have made notes, ask them to use these as the basis for extended writing, but emphasize that this need not be several pages long. Encourage them to use some of the words on the board, and stop the class occasionally to draw attention to interesting vocabulary choices and phrasing.

## Suggestion(s) for extension

Ask the children to use a thesaurus to find further words related to friendship. Some could prepare a presentation for the class or for a school assembly on the theme of friendship.

## Suggestion(s) for support

Ensure that those children who might struggle to find appropriate vocabulary or may have difficulty with spelling sit near to the wordbank which has been created on the board.

## Assessment opportunities

Look for evidence that children are able to write a sympathetic character sketch, using adverbs and adjectives appropriately.

## Opportunities for IT

Some of the children who experience difficulties might be asked to work on the computer using partially completed sentences and a wordbank to produce their own writing.

## Display ideas

Make a display entitled 'Friends' and mount the children's work on it. Intersperse the children's work with cards that have words related to friendship written on them. Provide some books which have descriptions of friendships and place them open at appropriate pages next to the display.

## Other aspects of the English PoS covered

Speaking and listening – 1a.

## Reference to photocopiable sheet

Photocopiable page 95 provides a writing frame to support children in writing a description of an actual or ideal 'best friend'.

# ANOTHER PLANET

*To plan and write imaginative extended stories.*

†† *Whole-class work followed by individual and group work.*

🕐 *At least one hour.*

## Previous skills/knowledge needed

Children will need to understand a little about the solar system and the planets, and about space travel.

## Key background information

In this activity children are asked to imagine life on another planet. The lesson could feature as English work during a term in which the focus of science lessons is 'the Earth in space'. It is important, given the fact that children will obviously not have visited other planets, that they should be given background information and be shown pictures, videos and other materials! However, they will probably have seen several science fiction films which show life on other planets.

*Trillions* by Nicholas Fisk (Hodder) tells the story of aliens from another planet who have come to Earth. This may be a useful book to read to the children in advance of the lesson. Point out to the children, if necessary, that aliens are intelligent creatures who are in a place from which they did not originate.

*Literacy Hour:* this activity could be appropriate for various year groups, depending upon the way it is structured. It may be particularly suitable for exploring and writing stories at Y4 T3 (T11, T12) and could lead into extended story writing (T13).

## Preparation

Gather together a selection of books, videos and other materials about planets or space exploration. Make an enlarged copy of photocopiable page 96. Discuss the theme of planets generally with the children and show them the books and videos that you have available so that they have an idea of what other planets in the solar system look like.

## Resources needed

Photocopiable page 96, books and videos about planets or space exploration, *Trillions* by Nicholas Fisk (optional), board or flip chart, paper, writing materials.

## What to do

*Introduction*

Begin by reading the story opening which appears on photocopiable page 96 with the children. Ask them what they think the space crew might find. Explain that the people who landed on the planet would be alien to any life forms that existed there. Discuss the way in which tension is created in the text.

Make a note of any vocabulary which might help the children in their independent writing, making a word list on the board. This might include: *alien, planet, explore, terrain, atmosphere, nervous, apprehensive, descend, ascend, extraterrestrial* and *voyage*.

## Individual/group work

Ask the children to continue the story, writing in the first person, and to describe what they find on the planet. Encourage them to be inventive and imaginative and to make up names for planets and life forms.

Some children may be able to plan their own complete stories. However, you may wish to provide some or all of the children with a structure for the beginning of the story. This could be as follows:

▲ Describe what you see from the space module.

▲ Describe the moment when you emerge from the space module.

▲ Describe what you feel when you step on to the land.

▲ Describe any sounds or smells.

▲ Do you have any other impressions?

▲ Describe an encounter with another life form.

Allow the children to develop their stories as they see fit after they have followed the structure for the first part.

## Suggestion(s) for extension

Some children could go on to produce short books using a desktop publishing package. Pictures could be scanned in and books could be bound by the children and placed in the school library.

## Suggestion(s) for support

For some children you may need to provide a more detailed structure which includes the beginnings of sentences and some key words which might be included.

## Assessment opportunities

Look for evidence that children are able to write extended stories based on story plans.

## Opportunities for IT

The children could reproduce extracts from their stories using the word processor and present them attractively for display. (Also, see 'Suggestion(s) for extension'.)

### Another planet

There was an air of trepidation in the cockpit as we descended slowly towards the planet which we had always called Zuron. The three of us, Mike, Becky and myself, looked at each other anxiously as we peered out of the hatches and saw the land appearing to rise towards us.

This was a new experience for all of us. Our previous voyages had taken us to known parts of the Solar System. We had only ever visited planets which had been visited before by people from Earth. This time it was different. We would be the first humans to set foot on Zuron. We looked down at the dry, barren land. Becky, the expert on other life forms, looked both anxious and excited. She desperately wanted to find signs of life but, like the rest of us, she was afraid that we might find enemies if we discovered anything.

Mike fired the remaining retro rockets and our descent slowed as the dust from the ground cascaded into the air blocking our view. Suddenly, with a thud and a rattle, we landed. The space module rocked alarmingly and then settled. Everything was still and quiet.

We looked through the hatches to see if the planet contained anything more interesting than rocks and sand. Each of our mouths fell open in unison and there was a collective gasp as a picture emerged through the settling dust.

## Display ideas

Extracts from the children's writing could be mounted on 'planets' which have been made by the children using papier mâché and balloons. These could be hung from the ceiling in front of a frieze of a space scene on which some examples of their extended writing have been displayed.

## Other aspects of the English PoS covered

Reading – 1d.
Speaking and listening – 2a.

## Reference to photocopiable sheet

Photocopiable page 96 provides a description of a space landing. It is the beginning of a science fiction story which the children can use as a starting point for their own stories, writing in a similar style.

# BILL'S NEW FROCK

***To write imaginatively in role.***

†† *Whole-class work followed by paired work.*

🕐 *At least one hour.*

## Previous skills/knowledge needed

Children will need to have read or be familiar with *Bill's New Frock* by Anne Fine (Mammoth).

## Key background information

In *Bill's New Frock*, Bill wakes up one morning to find that he is a girl. Anne Fine does not explain this phenomenon, but her story is a thought-provoking exploration of children's attitudes to gender and sexual stereotyping. This activity should encourage children to write from someone else's point of view. It may take place over a series of lessons, with different extracts being read from the story at the beginning of each, and different issues discussed and written about. It may even lead to the setting up of a class debate or it could become the basis of a class assembly.

*Literacy Hour:* for Y6 T1 this lesson could be developed into a series of Literacy Hours as follows:

▲ Hour 1: reading first chapter of *Bill's New Frock* and making notes on a typical day (T2, T3)

▲ Hour 2: reading another chapter, beginning writing of story with two narrators (T6)

▲ Hour 3: reading another chapter, continuing writing of story with two narrators (T6).

## Preparation

Read the story *Bill's New Frock* so that you are aware of the way in which Anne Fine uses the story as a vehicle for getting the reader to think about gender. Make one copy per pair of photocopiable page 97.

## Resources needed

*Bill's New Frock* by Anne Fine, photocopiable page 97, paper, board or flip chart, writing materials.

## What to do

*Introduction*

Read the first chapter of *Bill's New Frock* to the children and ask for their comments. In particular you might ask:

▲ How would you feel if you woke up to find that you were the opposite sex?

▲ What did Bill think?

▲ What would be the best and worst things about being a member of the opposite sex?

There is lots of scope for silliness here. You may need to begin by talking to the children about the need to behave in a mature and sensible way; it is important that they think seriously about the ways in which boys and girls may be treated differently.

Explain that you want them to think about a typical school day and that you would like them to make some notes in preparation for writing an imaginative piece describing a school day as a member of the opposite sex of the same age as themselves. Ask if they have noticed any ways in which boys and girls are treated differently or behave differently.

*Individual/group work*

Ask the children to work in pairs (one boy and one girl may be a good idea) to make notes under the different headings on the photocopiable sheet.

For subsequent lessons, ask the children to write in their pairs, with one assuming the role of a boy and one a girl. They should tell the story of the same day but should interpret events from their own point of view.

## Suggestion(s) for extension

Some children could go on to dramatize their writing and act out scenes from a day as a member of the opposite sex (after discussions with you about which scenes might be most suitable).

## Suggestion(s) for support

An adult helper could work with some children to record their ideas on the flip chart in order to help them to produce notes which would enable them to write at greater length later.

## Assessment opportunities

Look for evidence that children are able to write imaginatively in role.

## Display ideas

Display a copy of *Bill's New Frock* together with examples of the children's writing. You could divide the display board into two parts, with one half having the girls' points of view as written by the boys, and the other half having the boys' points of view written by the girls.

## Other aspects of the English PoS covered

Reading – 1d; 2b.

Speaking and listening – 2b.

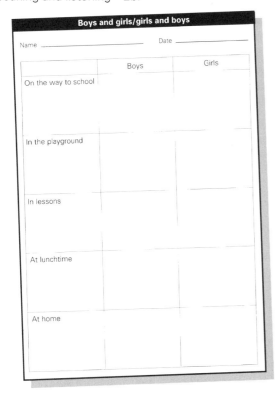

## Reference to photocopiable sheet

Photocopiable page 97 is a table which the children, working in pairs, can use to contrast the experiences of boys and girls during different parts of the school day.

# FLANNAN ISLE

***To write imaginatively in response to a stimulus.***
***To appreciate the use of unusual words in writing from the past.***

⫟ *Whole-class work followed by individual work.*
🕐 *At least one hour.*

## Key background information

*Flannan Isle* by Wilfred Wilson Gibson tells the story of a lighthouse with a mysterious past. In this activity the children look at the story which is told through the poem and then they are asked to write a continuation of the story which solves the mystery. The poem is rich in imagery and the poet's use of vocabulary should be discussed in detail.

*Literacy Hour:* this lesson could be the first of a series of Literacy Hours for Y5 in Term 2 which focus on different aspects of the text, including vocabulary, storyline, rhyming structure and poetic style. The children could go on to write poems and additional verses for poems (T12).

## Preparation

Look for some pictures of lighthouses, especially those set on islands. Make multiple copies of the poem 'Flannan Isle' on photocopiable pages 98 and 99, one for each child.

Read through the poem carefully and be prepared to discuss some of the more complex phrasing and vocabulary. You could write the following words on a large sheet of paper: *dwell, lee, glimmer, o'er, swell, gallant, blinded, dread, creek, crag, spurt, mazed, sun-blistered, threshold, spell, tongue-tied, ere, feeble, ransacked, cranny, cleft, nook, gaping, stole, steal, overtoppled, forsaken, befall, curs, flinching.*

Many of the words will be familiar to the children but they will be used to seeing them in different contexts, sometimes with different meanings.

## Resources needed

Photocopiable pages 98 and 99, list of words from poem (see 'Preparation'), paper, writing materials.

## What to do

### Introduction

Read the poem to the children as they follow the text, and then, after discussing its contents, read it again with them. Talk about the story which the poem tells and ask them to look for words and phrases which the poet has used to create a mysterious and eerie atmosphere. Look at the words in the context of the poem and discuss their meanings and how these might differ from those which the children usually associate with them. For example, *blinded* in the poem tells us that the light is not shining (as in 'behind a blind') rather than that someone has lost his or her sight, a *spell* means 'for a while' rather than having anything to do with words or witches, and *steal* refers to moving stealthily rather than robbery.

*Sun-blistered*, *tongue-tied* and *overtoppled* are probably self-explanatory, but a discussion about such terms could lead to children thinking of their own similar words.

### Individual/group work

Ask the children to make notes on what they think became of the lighthouse keepers. Encourage them to sustain the mood which Gibson created, and ask them to write the opening paragraph of a story (based on their notes) which begins with the three lighthouse keepers sitting at the table eating their meal.

## Suggestion(s) for extension

Ask the children to continue and complete the stories that they started in the individual/group work. Some children may attempt to write their stories in a poetic form similar to Gibson's, but initially they will almost certainly find it easier to use prose.

## Suggestion(s) for support

Work with a group of children who may need extra support to make notes to help them to write two opening lines for

a story that continues Gibson's poem. Use the children's suggestions to create a wordbank which they can draw upon when writing independently.

## Assessment opportunities

Look for evidence that children are able to convey feelings and moods through careful choice of words and phrases.

## Opportunities for IT

Some children could compose their opening paragraphs using the word processor.

## Display ideas

Display an enlarged copy of 'Flannan Isle', together with the children's opening paragraphs, on a background of a large frieze that shows a lighthouse on a barren island with waves crashing against the shore.

## Other aspects of the English PoS covered

Reading – 1d.
Speaking and listening – 2a.

## Reference to photocopiable sheets

Photocopiable pages 98 and 99 provide the poem 'Flannan Isle' by Wilfred Wilson Gibson, which is used to study the poet's use of vocabulary and to encourage the children to write imaginatively.

# THE FIB

**To write a story in the first person, using an episodic structure.**

†† *Whole-class work followed by individual work.*

🕐 *At least one hour.*

## Previous skills/knowledge needed

Children will need to understand what is meant by the first person and the third person in writing.

## Key background information

George Layton's story 'The Fib' in *The Fib and Other Stories* (Macmillan Children's Books) has captured the imagination of readers for many years. In it, a boy boasts to his friends that footballer Bobby Charlton is his uncle and the story hinges on a meeting with the player when the boy thinks he will be exposed. Bobby Charlton retired as a footballer many years ago and it may be necessary to substitute the name of a current player when telling the story.

The story is written in the first person and very much in the style of a child recounting the incidents.

*Literacy Hour:* this lesson could be part of a series of Literacy Hours for Y3 T3 which focus on writing stories. Other lessons could be used as starting points for various aspects of extended writing and could include: writing story openings (T11); writing in the first person (T12); using paragraphs to organize narrative (T13); using words to signal time sequences (S6); using speech marks (S4).

## Preparation

Find some pictures of a famous Manchester United football player. This could be Bobby Charlton or it could be a current player if you intend to adapt the story. Display the pictures prior to the lesson. Make multiple copies of part of the story (if your school has a CLA licence), one copy for each child or pair – the first two pages would be ideal as they set the tone for the story's style. (NB Manchester United may not be the children's favourite team, but since the club is featured in the story, it would be difficult to substitute another local team without careful reading.)

## Resources needed

Pictures of a Manchester United player, *The Fib* by George Layton, copies of part of the story (see 'Preparation'), paper, writing materials. Cassette player and blank cassettes for support activity.

## What to do

### Introduction

Discuss telling the truth and telling lies with the children and ask them if they have ever made something up which subsequently caused them problems. Explain that in the story which you are going to read to them a boy's fib eventually causes him great anxiety. The story has a happy

ending, but you may wish to stress that this is not usually the case when people tell lies.

Read the story to the children, then distribute copies of part of it and look at the text with them. There are some examples of colloquialisms and the phrasing is reminiscent of a child's conversation from parts of northern England. Look at phrases such as *Oh heck, Don't be such a jessie* and *Blooming daft this* and discuss the way in which George Layton has used them to introduce humour and to show that it is a child who is telling the story.

### Individual/group work

Ask the children to think of a fib that they may have told or to think about one similar to that in the story. Explain that they are going to write stories about the consequences of telling a fib. Show them how they could begin by writing an opening sentence for a story in the first person. Ask them to write in the first person throughout their stories.

Encourage children to plan their stories and to make brief notes of the structure. They could divide their stories into, say, six parts and then make notes for each part or episode. You will need to stop the class occasionally to discuss progress, to read parts of stories aloud, and to provide spellings of words which children may need.

Provide a checklist for the children to use when proofreading their work and include in it an instruction to 'Check that you have kept to the first person throughout your story' or similar.

## Suggestion(s) for extension

Some children could read more of George Layton's stories, for example the second volume of short stories about the same children – *The Swap and Other Stories* (Macmillan Children's Books). They could go on to make notes for a piece of drama based upon one of the stories and use them to present an improvisation to the rest of the class.

## Suggestion(s) for support

Since the stories closely resemble written speech, some children could make brief notes for their stories before using their notes to record their stories onto tape. They could then be helped by other children or by an adult to turn their oral stories into written ones.

## Assessment opportunities

Look for evidence that children are able to write stories consistently using the first person. Note, too, their ability to organize their stories into a sequence of episodes.

## Opportunities for IT

Some children could write their stories using the word processor, although many will find it difficult to write at length on the computer at this stage. An alternative might be for them to compose introductions or endings using the word processor and then handwrite the rest of their stories.

## Display ideas

Display George Layton's books together with copies of the children's stories. The children could mount their work onto folded pieces of card so that it appears in booklet form and can be taken away from the display to be read. Alternatively, they could be attached to the wall so that all the children have access to read them.

## Other aspects of the English PoS covered

Reading – 1d.
Speaking and listening – 3a.

# CHANGING PLACES

*To write an imaginative story, possibly with two different narrators.*

†† *Whole-class work followed by individual or paired work.*

🕐 *At least one hour.*

## Previous skills/knowledge needed

Children will need to have experienced stories in which characters change places (see below).

## Key background information

This activity is based upon the premise of two people exchanging roles. There have been some notable examples in fiction of such a theme being used. The children may have seen the film *Freaky Friday* or the television serialization *Vice Versa* (based on the book by F Anstey). You may wish to follow up the activity 'Bill's New Frock' (page 26) with this activity.

*Literacy Hour:* this activity could be developed for most age groups at Key Stage 2, but may be particularly suited to Y6 T1 (T7) and could form part of a series of Literacy Hours which explore planning of stories.

## Preparation

Find a copy of a story in which characters change places, for example E Nesbit's 'The Cathood of Maurice' from *The Magic World* (Puffin), or *The Magic Finger* by Roald Dahl (Puffin).

## Resources needed

A copy of a story (see 'Preparation'), paper, writing materials.

## What to do

*Introduction*

Read an extract from a story in which people change places, and ask the children questions such as: if it were possible, who would they wish to change places with for a day? Do they think they would like to change places with anyone permanently?

Talk with the children about their answers and ask them to suggest some things which they might do if they were someone else for the day.

*Individual/group work*

Explain that the children are going to plan a story in which they change places with someone else for a day. They could write from the point of view of each of the two characters by juxtaposing sections telling each person's story.

Encourage them to be adventurous both in their use of language and in the ideas which they include in their stories.

## FIVE-WORD STORIES

*To build a story around five key words. To be able to arrive at the best uses of words for different purposes.*

†† *Whole-class work followed by individual work.*

🕐 *At least one hour.*

### Previous skills/knowledge needed

Children will need to understand that some words can be used as different parts of speech.

### Key background information

In this activity children are asked to build a short piece of writing around five words. They will need to understand the different ways in which the words may be used. Many words can be used as different parts of speech. For example, the word *down* could be a verb (as in *down a drink*), a noun (as in *the down on a duckling*) a preposition (as in *put it down*) or an adjective (as in *The players were down after the bad result*).

*Literacy Hour:* word-level work could be done on parts of speech if this activity were to be used as part of a series of Literacy Hours. It could also be developed into a series of Literacy Hours for Y4 T2 around the themes of using words for different purposes and turning brief notes into connected prose (T22).

### Suggestion(s) for extension

Some children could go on to write at greater length and to turn their work into short books which could be illustrated and bound by the children, before becoming part of the class or school library.

### Suggestion(s) for support

Encourage children to get their ideas down quickly and emphasize that at the planning stage this is more important than accuracy. However, you should also encourage them to review their planning and to look for words which they think they may have misspelled. They could underline these and show them to you. You could then provide a list of correctly spelled words which children found difficult, as an aid for their independent writing.

### Assessment opportunities

Look for evidence that children are able to use a narrative style and can produce lively, imaginative writing. Do they show an awareness of viewpoint?

### Opportunities for IT

Invite children to reproduce excerpts from their stories for display using the word processor. They could use different fonts to represent the two narrative viewpoints.

### Display ideas

Display excerpts from the children's stories together with examples of published fiction which has a theme of changing places (see opposite page).

### Other aspects of the English PoS covered

Reading – 1d.
Speaking and listening – 2a.

### Preparation

Prepare a set of about 20 cards with words written on them. The words could be different parts of speech and might include ones that you have used in a previous spelling lesson.

### Resources needed

A set of word cards (see 'Preparation'), board or flip chart, paper, writing materials.

### What to do

*Introduction*

Explain that you have a selection of words written on cards and that you are going to ask the class to help you to write a story using five randomly selected words, each of which must appear at least once in the story. Try doing this orally before selecting five further words and modelling writing a story on the board, using the children's suggestions. If any of the words could be used in different ways, for instance as a verb and as a noun, discuss this with the children and encourage them to use the words as different parts of speech.

*Individual/group work*

Invite children from each group to come to the front of the class and choose five cards from the set which has been placed face down. When five have been selected, write the words on the board and discuss their spellings. Explain that the children are now going to write their own stories and that these may be as long as they wish but they should include all five of the words somewhere in them.

Encourage them to plan their stories first and to make notes so that they can decide where each word might appear in their text.

## Suggestion(s) for extension

Children could be given sets of word cards and be asked to choose, say, three at random and then write a paragraph which includes each of them. They could go on to add words to the set and invite friends to use them as a basis for writing.

## Suggestion(s) for support

Do lots of oral work with those children who might struggle with the writing and make sure that they are familiar with at least the five words which are to be used as the basis for the stories. Some could work with more able partners to produce joint pieces of writing.

## Assessment opportunities

Look for evidence that children understand that some words can be used in many different ways. Note their ability to turn brief notes in the form of five words into connected prose.

## Display ideas

Display examples of the children's written work and mount word cards around them. Ask children to find the words around which they think each story was built.

## Other aspects of the English PoS covered

Reading – 1d.
Speaking and listening – 1a.

# CARTOONS WITH CAPTIONS

**To be able to write suitable captions for cartoon pictures.**

†† *Whole-class work followed by individual and paired/group work.*

🕐 *At least one hour.*

## Previous skills/knowledge needed

Children will need to have seen examples of cartoons and their captions.

## Key background information

In this activity children are asked to look at a selection of cartoons and to make up appropriate and humorous captions.

## Preparation

Make a collection of cartoons from children's comics which you think will appeal to the children. All but one of the cartoons should have the caption covered up, and there should be enough cartoons without captions for each member of the class to have one.

## Resources needed

A collection of cartoons (see 'Preparation'), board or flip chart, writing materials.

## What to do

### Introduction

Show the children a cartoon which you think will appeal to their sense of humour. Let them look at it individually and discuss the caption, asking the children if they have seen similar cartoons. Now show them another cartoon, but this time cover the caption and ask them to suggest captions of their own. Explain that their captions should be short and to the point – and they should be funny. Show them how they can edit and redraft the captions to improve them. Write some of their suggestions on the board and then reveal the original and ask them which they preferred. Repeat the exercise with some other cartoons until you feel that the children are confident about the activity. Show them that cartoon captions are usually written in block capitals and that lower-case writing is rarely used.

### Individual/group work

Give out sufficient cartoons for the children to have one each, but explain that they are going to work in pairs or threes to write captions for the cartoons. Encourage them to revise and edit their captions and to discuss them with their colleagues. If they finish their captions, they could exchange them with others or be given more by you.

Bring the class together and show the children some of the cartoons and captions and ask for constructive criticism as well as different ideas.

### Suggestion(s) for extension

Children could produce their own cartoons or could use cartoon strips to write captions for each of a series of pictures.

### Suggestion(s) for support

For some children, you could provide a set of cartoons and a set of captions and ask them to match each to the other.

### Assessment opportunities

Look for evidence that children are able to write concisely and in a style appropriate for cartoons.

### Display ideas

Display the cartoons, together with a range of different captions for each one, alongside cartoons taken from newspapers and magazines.

### Other aspects of the English PoS covered

Speaking and listening – 1a.

## HEADLINES

***To make use of the contents of newspaper reports to write eye-catching headlines.***

†† *Whole-class work followed by individual and group work.*

🕐 *At least one hour.*

### Previous skills/knowledge needed

Children will need to be familiar with newspaper headlines.

### Key background information

Newspaper headlines tend to be eye-catching and should draw potential readers to them. Some newspapers such as *The Sun* and *The Sport* have even produced books which consist solely of their headlines. Many tabloid papers have headlines which exceed in size the articles that follow them. This activity focuses on newspaper articles and their headlines and encourages the children to read articles carefully before making up appropriate headlines for them.

*Literacy Hour:* this activity could be used as part of a series of Literacy Hours for Y4 in T1 with a focus upon looking at the features of newspapers (T20, T21, T24).

### Preparation

Make a collection of newspaper headlines. Tabloid papers are a rich source, but you may need to be cautious about the content of some. Sunday supplements, especially *The Observer* and *The Sunday Independent,* and other types of magazine, often contain headlines which are full of puns and plays on words. In addition, collect some articles with the headlines removed and kept separately.

### Resources needed

Newspapers, newspaper and magazine headlines and articles (see 'Preparation'), paper, writing materials.

### What to do

#### Introduction

Show the children the headlines you have collected (including the ones which have their accompanying articles put aside) and ask them if they can predict from reading them what might be in the stories. Next, read some of the short articles and ask the children to look at your collection of headlines and decide which headlines would go with the articles. Discuss headlines which exaggerate and sensationalize, as well as those which are rather bland. You might include some of those which appear in property guides *(Three-bed semi in Quiet Street; Detached house near to station; Bungalow in cul-de-sac)* as well as examples from tabloids.

#### Individual/group work

Provide the children with several unheaded newspaper articles for each group and ask them to work together to read the articles and to devise appropriate headlines. At this stage they should not be producing large-sized headings but should simply jot their ideas down.

When they feel happy with their headlines, ask them to check their spellings carefully before using the word processor to produce headlines using different fonts and font sizes.

### Suggestion(s) for extension
Some children could exchange headlines and then write appropriate articles to accompany them, before comparing these with the originals.

### Suggestion(s) for support
The children could work with writing partners to produce headlines, particularly where one of the pair has difficulties reading the text.

### Assessment opportunities
Look for evidence that children can understand the organization of newspaper articles and headlines, and that they are able to write and present headlines in an appropriate style.

### Opportunities for IT
A word processor could be used to design headlines in large fonts to display with the articles (see 'Individual/group work').

### Display ideas
Display real newspapers, together with some of the children's headlines and any examples of articles that they wrote in the extension activity to go with the headlines.

### Other aspects of the English PoS covered
Reading – 1b.
Speaking and listening – 1c.

## JESSICA'S OTHER HOUSE

*To plan, draft, revise, proofread and present an imaginative story based upon the theme of a parallel world.*

✝✝ *Whole-class work followed by individual and group work.*

🕐 *At least one hour.*

### Previous skills/knowledge needed
Children will need to be aware of some of the stories from the same genre as 'Jessica's other house' (see photocopiable pages 100 and 101). This activity links to 'Another world' on page 32 of *Curriculum Bank Writing, Key Stage 2*.

### Key background information
This activity features a familiar theme in children's literature: travel into a parallel world. You may have read the Narnia stories by CS Lewis (HarperCollins), *A Stitch in Time* by Penelope Lively (Mammoth) and Lewis Carroll's *Alice's Adventures in Wonderland* or *Through the Looking Glass* (Puffin). In these books and many more, children are transported into a different world or time and have adventures there.

'Jessica's other house' is the beginning of a story which features in two other activities in this book: 'The broken window' (see page 13) and 'Girls don't play football' (see page 15).

*Literacy Hour:* this lesson could be used as a Literacy Hour for Y5 in Term 1 and as a starting point for extended writing. Further Literacy Hours could focus on different aspects of story writing, including paragraphs (T15), dialogue (S7), the use of similes and metaphors (T17) and adjectives and adverbs (T16).

### Preparation
Find examples of stories which involve parallel worlds, and make copies of photocopiable pages 100 and 101.

## Resources needed

Photocopiable pages 100 and 101, paper, writing materials.

## What to do

*Introduction*

Discuss with the children some examples of stories which involve parallel worlds and ask them about the devices which authors use to transport their characters from one world to another. Explain that the story which you are about to introduce has a similar theme.

Read the story with the children and ask them questions such as:

▲ How did Jessica travel from one world to another?

▲ What kind of house did she live in?

▲ How could she tell she was in a different house after she climbed down the ladder?

▲ How do you think she felt when she heard the voice?

Now ask the children to spend a few minutes jotting down their ideas for what happens next, and how the story might continue.

*Individual/group work*

Ask the children to plan, then draft their stories. Encourage them to try to maintain the style of the writing and to be imaginative in their ideas about the continuation of the story. Explain that they should write at some length and should not try to end the story at this stage.

This activity could be developed into an extended writing lesson or series of lessons, with children writing further chapters for the story. Encourage the introduction of new characters and of dialogue.

## Suggestion(s) for extension

Some children may be asked to create their own stories of people entering other worlds. They could also be asked to investigate the features of a number of such published stories and record their opinions on them.

## Suggestion(s) for support

Some children may need a great deal of support if they are to have the confidence to produce pieces of sustained writing. Provide them with banks of useful words such as *entered, explore, search, extraordinary, bizarre, weird, curious* and *uncertain*. Ensure that the children have plenty of opportunities to discuss their own and other people's work.

## Assessment opportunities

Look for evidence that children are able to plan and draft their writing and write in an appropriate style for an extended story.

## Opportunities for IT

Some children could use the word processor to plan, draft and revise their stories, before presenting finished

versions. These can then be printed out and bound to make printed books, perhaps with the addition of illustrations.

## Display ideas

Display the opening to 'Jessica's other house' together with the children's versions of the next part of the story. Display examples of other stories that involve parallel worlds alongside the writing and encourage children to read these by leaving them open or bookmarked at exciting sections.

## Other aspects of the English PoS covered

Reading – 1d.

Speaking and listening – 1a.

## Reference to photocopiable sheets

Photocopiable pages 100 and 101 shows the opening of an imaginative story which the children can read, discuss and continue.

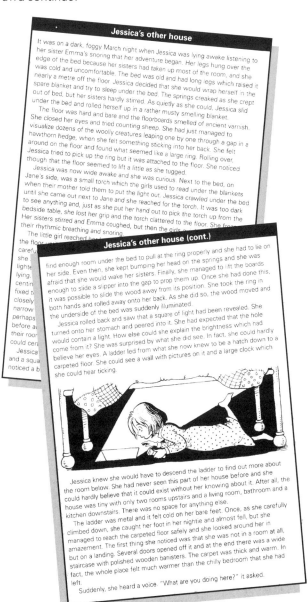

# CINQUAINS

*To write a poem in a given format and to understand what a syllable is.*

†† *Whole-class work followed by individual or paired work.*

🕐 *At least one hour.*

## Previous skills/knowledge needed

Children will need to understand syllables. It may be useful to use this activity as a follow-up to work on haiku. These are featured in the activity 'Haiku' on page 46 of *Curriculum Bank Writing, Key Stage 2*.

## Key background information

Cinquains are five-line poems with a standard syllable pattern as follows:

> 2 on the first line,
> 4 on the second,
> 6 on the third,
> 8 on the fourth,
> 2 on the fifth.

For example:

> How mean
> To ask poor me
> To write you a cinquain
> When I cannot even pronounce
> Cinquain.

> I love
> To hear the sound
> Of happy young children
> Dashing around the school playground
> Yelling.

> Never
> Keep your shoes on
> When you get into bed
> Because you will make the clean sheets
> Dirty.

This activity provides an opportunity to discuss syllables, as well as a chance for children to write simple structured poetry.

*Literacy Hour:* this activity could form part of a series of Literacy Hours for Y4 at Term 3 (T5, T14) which focus on poems with different styles and structures.

## Preparation

Make up some examples of cinquains. If you do this yourself it will help you to appreciate the problems which the children may encounter. Make an enlarged copy of the cinquains so that the whole class can read them.

## Resources needed

Examples of cinquains, paper, writing materials.

## What to do

*Introduction*

Read some examples of cinquains to the children and ask them to try to work out what the rule is for their structure. Talk about syllables and write out the rule with the children's help.

Ask them to help you to write some more cinquains, and model the layout for them. When their suggestions for lines do not conform to the syllable pattern, write them down anyway and then ask the class to look at the lines and decide if they need to be adjusted. It is an important part of the activity that children should edit and revise the poems as they write them and should learn that the d e l e t i o n, substitution or insertion of words can help to make the poems follow the rules.

*Individual/group work*

Explain that you would like the children to write their own cinquains. You might wish to concentrate on a particular theme such as the weather, or you may decide that children should choose their own subjects. They may write as many as they like, but they should concentrate on trying to make them as good as possible and should revise and edit them until they feel proud of their efforts. Stop the class occasionally to read examples of successful cinquains and to discuss any problems.

## Suggestion(s) for extension

Some children could go on to attempt to write haiku, which have five syllables on the first line, seven on the second and five on the third.

## Suggestion(s) for support

Some children may need to be helped to produce a list of common words under headings which state how many syllables they have. This could provide a wordbank to help them with their writing. For example:

| one-syllable words | two-syllable words | three-syllable words |
| --- | --- | --- |
| I | happy | wandering |
| am | falling | delightful |
| rain | garden | understand |

## Assessment opportunities

Look for evidence that children understand the concept of syllables and that they can recognize syllabic patterns in multi-syllabic words. Note their abilities to use the structure of the cinquain and to revise their work by adding, substituting or deleting words.

## Opportunities for IT

This activity could be done on the word processor by some children. This would allow them to edit their poems to achieve the correct syllable pattern without constant rewriting.

## Display ideas

Display the children's poems together with appropriate illustrations. You might also provide some examples of other poems which have syllabic structures, such as haiku.

## Other aspects of the English PoS covered

Reading – 1d.
Speaking and listening – 1a.

## TRIOLETS

*To write a poem in a given format and to understand that repetition can be a useful device in poetry. To use rhymes correctly.*

†† *Whole-class work followed by individual or paired work.*

⏱ *At least one hour.*

### Previous skills/knowledge needed

Children will need to have had experience of poems which feature repetition.

### Key background information

Triolets are structured poems in which the first line reappears as the fourth and seventh and the second reappears as the eighth. For example:

> Writing poetry is fun,
> An easy task for anyone,
> It's simply great.
> Writing poetry is fun,
> When Miss says, 'Poems, everyone!'
> I just can't wait.
> Writing poetry is fun,
> An easy task for anyone.

*Literacy Hour:* this lesson could be part of a series of Literacy Hours for Y3 T2 which focus on rhythms and repetition (T4, T11). Sentence-level work on capitalization for new lines in poetry and subject–verb agreement could be incorporated (S8).

## Resources needed
Examples of triolets, photocopiable page 102, board or flip chart, paper, writing materials.

## What to do
### Introduction
Introduce triolets by reading some examples and asking the children if they can work out the pattern for writing them. Once the pattern has been established, ask the children to help you to write a triolet. You might include the name of a child in it. A starting point could be an incomplete triolet, with only the first line given (this should include one of the children's names or the name of a famous person).

Make a point of looking at rhyming couplets and sets of rhyming words which could be used. Write these on the board and talk about the ways in which they are spelled. Show the children how they can work out rhymes orally by taking the rime of a word, say -ish, and going through the alphabet trying each letter as an onset until they have a collection of possible rhymes. They can then check in a dictionary to see which ones are real words. For example: *bish, cish, dish, fish, gish, hish…*

### Individual/group work
Ask the children to begin by using photocopiable page 102 as a way of giving them a structure and some starting points for their own poems. Encourage them to look for rhymes, but allow them to produce triolets without rhymes if they find this too difficult. Once they have completed a poem, you or another adult or other children could help with suggestions for rhymes.

When the children feel sufficiently confident, ask them to produce complete triolets without the aid of the photocopiable sheet.

## Preparation
Make one copy per child of photocopiable page 102. Write some sample triolets and enlarge them so that the children will be able to read them. You might like to base them on the ones below, substituting the names of members of your class for those in the poems.

> David Dean read lots of books.
> His friends all gave him funny looks.
> He couldn't put them down.
> David Dean read lots of books.
> He brought them home in a fleet of trucks,
> From the library in town.
> David Dean read lots of books.
> His friends all gave him funny looks.

> Louise McCarthy sits in front of me,
> She's the kind of girl I'd like to be.
> She has long hair.
> Louise McCarthy sits in front of me,
> I'd really like to ask her home for tea.
> I wouldn't dare.
> Louise McCarthy sits in front of me,
> She's the kind of girl I'd like to be.

> Whenever things go wrong, it's always Steve.
> He gets in trouble you would not believe,
> He's just not cool.
> Whenever things go wrong, it's always Steve.
> Our teacher says he's managed to achieve
> Sheer havoc in our school.
> Whenever things go wrong, it's always Steve.
> He gets in trouble you would not believe.

## Suggestion(s) for extension
Read through some of the children's poems and talk about scansion. Ask the children to look at some poems to see how poets maintain rhythm by keeping the same number of syllables in lines which form pairs or groups of lines. Encourage them to look again at their own poems and revise them in the light of their findings.

## Suggestion(s) for support
Some children may need to work with partners to produce poems. However, everyone should be encouraged to contribute to the poems and less able children should not merely be scribes or passive partners.

## Assessment opportunities

Look for evidence that children are able to write structured poems in a given format. Look, too, at children's spelling choices when creating rhymes. Do they make choices which are possible or do they need help with spelling rules? You may need to follow up the lesson by looking at rules such as: 'English words do not end with v', 'English words do not end with j'.

## Opportunities for IT

The repetitious nature of the poems lends itself very well to the use of the word processor, since children can 'copy' and 'paste' lines and save themselves time in typing poems out. Encourage them to compose poems on the computer and to present them attractively, using a range of fonts.

## Display ideas

Display an enlarged triolet with arrows from labels to some of the lines. On the labels write the features of triolets, for example 'The first line reappears as the fourth and seventh', 'The second line reappears as the eighth'.

## Other aspects of the English PoS covered

Reading – 1d.
Speaking and listening – 1a.

## Reference to photocopiable sheet

Photocopiable page 102 shows some incomplete poems in the triolet form which the children can complete before going on to create their own similar poems.

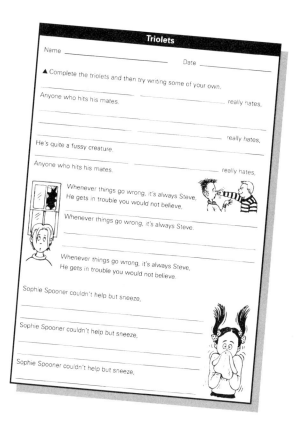

# CHARACTER SKETCHES

*To write character sketches.*

†† *Whole-class work followed by individual or paired work.*

🕒 *At least one hour.*

## Key background information

The photocopiable sheet provides an example of a negative character sketch of a pirate and a positive character sketch of a woman.

*Literacy Hour:* this lesson could form part of a series of Literacy Hours for Y4 T1 which focus on character descriptions (T1, T2, T11).

## Preparation

Find some examples of character sketches – these may be taken from both fiction and non-fiction. Present them as a display and show them to the children. Make an enlarged copy of the character sketches on photocopiable page 103.

In advance of the lesson, ask the children to find out as much as they can about a person they really like and one whom they do not like. (The latter, in particular, should not be anyone who is part of the school or who lives locally.) The children could choose a well-known fictional character such as Victor Hazell from *Danny the Champion of the World* by Roald Dahl (Puffin) or the White Witch from *The Lion, the Witch and the Wardrobe* by CS Lewis (HarperCollins).

## Resources needed

Photocopiable page 103, other character sketches, board or flip chart, paper, writing materials.

## What to do

*Introduction*

Read the character sketch of Jim Baker with the children and ask them what they think about the pirate. Next, read the character sketch of Joan Dix and ask for their opinions. Encourage them to comment on how the style of each

piece affects the reader's view of the character. Explain that the descriptions are examples of character sketches and that they are going to write their own descriptions of people. They could write about well-known people or they could make up characters. Emphasize to the children that character sketches need not be wholly negative or positive and that they could include both good and bad points about their subjects.

### Individual/group work

Ask the children to write character sketches individually or in pairs. You may wish to ask them to be concise, and you could limit the number of words or ask them to confine their descriptions to a single page. Encourage the children to draft and refine their work and to avoid repeating words.

Allow them a short period to discuss their character sketches and to plan them, before stopping the class and inviting the children to ask you for help with any words which they do not feel confident about spelling. Encourage everyone to suggest spellings and write them on the board, before discussing correct spellings. By doing this, you will be modelling for the children an approach to working out spellings independently.

The children's character sketches could be shared with the rest of the class and this could be developed into a game, with children reading out their character sketches and asking the other children to guess who they are writing about.

### Suggestion(s) for extension

Some children could be responsible for compiling and editing a class book of character sketches of famous people. This could be placed in the class library.

### Suggestion(s) for support

Some children may lack knowledge of their chosen character. Be prepared to help them to produce a positive character sketch of a well-known person by having brief notes available to supplement their own ideas.

### Assessment opportunities

Look for evidence that children are able to write character sketches which evoke sympathy or dislike, or a mixture of both.

### Opportunities for IT

Some children could use a word processor to draft, revise and design their character sketches. They could use the Internet or a CD-ROM to obtain pictures of their characters, if these are available; alternatively, they could scan in their own sketches.

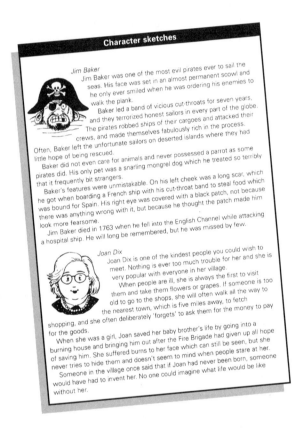

### Display ideas

See 'Suggestion(s) for extension'.

### Other aspects of the English PoS covered

Reading – 1c.

Speaking and listening – 1a.

### Reference to photocopiable sheet

Photocopiable page 103 presents two character sketches – one unsympathetic, the other sympathetic – which the children can discuss and use as models for their own sketches of real or imaginary characters.

# ALTERNATIVE ENDINGS

**_To write an alternative ending for a story._**

**††** _Whole-class work followed by individual or paired work._

🕐 _At least one hour._

## Previous skills/knowledge needed
Children will need to be aware of a range of story endings.

## Key background information
Roald Dahl's _Revolting Rhymes_ (Puffin) provides excellent examples of alternative versions of familiar stories. In this activity children are asked to consider stories which are well known to them and write alternative endings for them.

_Literacy Hour:_ this activity could be a Literacy Hour for Y4 T3 (T12) and could be followed by opportunities for extended writing of longer story endings or complete stories (T13).

## Preparation
Find a selection of well-known stories with which the children are familiar. This could include traditional tales such as 'The Three Little Pigs' or 'Sleeping Beauty', moral tales such as 'The Boy Who Cried Wolf', legends such as 'The Pied Piper of Hamelin', or modern stories by authors such as Roald Dahl.

## Resources needed
A selection of well-known stories, paper, writing materials.

## What to do
_Introduction_
Show the children the stories that you have collected and ask them to tell you a little about some of them. Ask them to talk about the characters, the plots and the endings. Focus in particular on the endings and invite the children to make suggestions for different ways in which the stories might have been concluded.

_Individual/group work_
Ask the children to choose one of the stories that you showed to them and make notes on an alternative ending, in preparation for writing at greater length. They should then turn their notes into prose and write a story ending. Encourage them to be imaginative in their responses, and ask them to ensure that their readers will know what happened to each of the main characters.

## Suggestion(s) for extension
Some children may wish to write alternative endings for their own favourite stories rather than those that you showed them in the introductory session.

## Suggestion(s) for support
Some children may need to begin the activity with a shared writing session with the teacher, using the board or a flip chart. Provide word lists as a resource for the children to draw upon. The lists could include words which are specific to some of the stories, as well as more general words such as _climax, finally, ultimately, suddenly_ and _happily._

## Assessment opportunities
Look for evidence that children are able to draw upon the original stories when writing their alternative endings, and for signs that they are able to write in an appropriate style for a story.

## Opportunities for IT
Key in a well-known story and make multiple copies of it. Ask the children to take turns to add their own endings, and then print them out to be collated and bound into a book. The stories could also be left on file for others to read at the computer, perhaps selecting them by page from a contents list that indicates the different types of ending.

## Display ideas
Display story books together with a wall display of the children's alternative endings.

## Other aspects of the English PoS covered
Reading – 1d.
Speaking and listening – 1a.

# Non-fiction writing

The activities in this chapter are intended to broaden children's awareness of the range of styles of non-fiction writing. These include newspaper reporting, letter writing, design of certificates and advertisements, reference book entries, work based on charts and autobiography.

The children are provided with various stimuli which are intended to invoke real-life situations and relate their writing to that which they will encounter outside school.

Most of the activities can be undertaken within a single lesson, but may also be developed so that children are given opportunities for extended writing. 'The town' activities, for example (see pages 57–61), can be spread over several lessons and become part of an ongoing class activity which is related to other areas of the curriculum.

It is important throughout all non-fiction work that children are provided with plenty of opportunities to see and read examples of published texts, and teachers are encouraged to find these in addition to making use of the photocopiable sheets.

As with most aspects of writing, children should feel that they have an audience for what they have written. The activities within this chapter lend themselves to display and publication, and there are several opportunities for writing to be done using word processing so that high-quality presentation can be achieved.

## WHO'S WHO

*To write in a style appropriate for a reference book.*

†† *Whole-class work followed by individual and paired work.*

🕐 *At least one hour.*

### Previous skills/knowledge needed
Children will need to be aware of abbreviations and the formats of reference sources.

### Key background information
This activity focuses on the writing of entries for a reference book – the need for brevity in this type of writing and the importance of knowing the meaning of abbreviations that are often included.

*Literacy Hour:* this activity could be linked to a series of Literacy Hours for Y6 in Term 1 on the theme of biographical and autobiographical reading and writing (T11, T14).

### Preparation
Find a variety of reference books which provide brief biographical details of well-known people, such as *Who's Who*, so that you can discuss the format and style of the writing. The pen portraits which appear in programmes for sporting events and theatre are a good source.

### Resources needed
Various biographical reference sources, paper, board or flip chart, writing materials.

### What to do
*Introduction*

Show the children the biographical reference texts which you have collected, distributing them to different groups of children so that they can see the general layout and writing style.

Look closely at one of the books and choose an entry for a person who is well known to all the children. Discuss any abbreviations (including acronyms) that are given, writing them on the board, and talk with the children about the way in which punctuation marks, such as apostrophes and full stops, can be used in abbreviations (for example *OBE* – Officer of the Order of the British Empire, *Capt.* – Captain, *T'ham* – Tottenham).

Ask the children if one of them would like to volunteer to have his or her own biographical details written by the class. Go through different aspects of the person's interests and experiences, and model writing an entry for a class 'Who's Who' with the help of the children, writing notes on the board.

### Individual/group work

Ask the children to write 'Who's Who' entries for each other, after they have discussed with a partner the things which should be included. Encourage them to begin by making notes and then drafting, revising and editing them until they have a final copy (this can be proofread by the person who is described).

Stop the class occasionally to share ideas and to ensure that children are able to follow the format of a 'Who's Who' entry.

### Suggestion(s) for extension

Some children could go on to produce biographical notes for well-known local, national and international celebrities. Ask them to research the characters carefully and to make notes before they write their entries.

### Suggestion(s) for support

Provide those children who might find this activity difficult with some incomplete sentences which they can complete as a starting point for their entries. For example, they might have:

_____ was born in _____.
His/her hobbies include _____ , _____ and _____.
His/her family comprises _____ , _____ , _____
and _____.

### Assessment opportunities

Look for evidence that children are able to write in a style appropriate to reference books.

### Opportunities for IT

A database could be created by some children, making use of the entries for the whole class. This could then be used as a source of information which could be used in other lessons such as mathematics for data handling work.

### Display ideas

Make a class 'Who's Who' and display it prominently, preferably next to a copy of the published version and other similar reference books.

### Other aspects of the English PoS covered

Reading – 1b.
Speaking and listening – 1a.

## MAKING TEXTBOOKS

**To understand the structure of a textbook.**

†† *Whole-class work followed by group and individual work.*

⏲ *At least one hour.*

### Previous skills/knowledge needed

Children will need to understand the format of textbooks and know how to use sections which can help them to locate information such as contents and indexes.

### Key background information

In this activity children create an information book for a topic which they are currently studying. The activity should help them to understand the features of textbooks so that they find it easier to read for information.

*Literacy Hour:* while the time taken to produce the book will exceed that available in individual Literacy Hours, you may wish to devote a series of Literacy Hours (for Y5 T2) to different features of texts and ask the children to produce their work during group sessions and develop it at other times. The work could include exploring a range of textbooks as well as composing one (T15, T16, T17, T22).

### Preparation

Gather together a wide selection of non-fiction texts relevant to a current class topic or area of study. Make a display of the anatomy of a textbook either by photocopying pages such as the index, title page, contents, glossary, publisher's blurb and so on, or by cutting up a textbook which would otherwise be too damaged to use.

### Resources needed

A range of textbooks and a display of the anatomy of a textbook (see 'Preparation'), materials for making books, collections of illustrations (picture collections from the computer would be useful, if available), writing materials.

### What to do

*Introduction*

Introduce the children to a simple textbook and discuss its features. Show them similar features in books on the textbook display. If you are undertaking a series of lessons, concentrate on a different feature during each introductory session.

Discuss, in particular, the elements of a textbook which make it easy to use. For example, show the children how they can use an index or a contents page to help them to locate information quickly.

*Individual/group work*

Explain to the children that the whole class will be making a textbook for their current topic or area of study and that, because it is such a big job, there will be a division of labour, with different people producing different parts of the book. You might allocate tasks as follows:

▲ Research – everyone taking part at first, but some children concentrating on this throughout a series of lessons, making notes for others to write up or word-process. (Divide up the different aspects of the topic so that different children become 'experts' in different areas.)

▲ Writing up – one group in charge of converting others' notes into final copy.

▲ Editing – some children organizing and refining the text.

All children may be involved in each aspect of the book's production at some time and everyone should have an opportunity to work on the index and contents pages, as an understanding of these is essential for their own research.

When the book is nearing completion, some children could begin work as illustrators and designers while others create the cover.

## Suggestion(s) for extension

Invite the children to go on to work independently to make their own textbooks (they could do this both in school and at home). This could be an ongoing project that involves children in making use of secondary sources.

## Suggestion(s) for support

Provide wordbanks and copies of simple reference texts on the subject and encourage the children to make use of these to support their independent writing.

## Assessment opportunities

Look for evidence that children understand the structures of non-fiction texts and are able both to read and compose features such as contents and indexes.

## Opportunities for IT

This activity is well-suited to desktop publishing. You may wish to have all parts of the book produced on the computer by children taking turns after the draft has been mainly written by hand. Illustrations could be scanned in from the children's drawings.

## Display ideas

Include finished books as part of the class or school library. You may wish to make additional copies for children to take home.

## Other aspects of the English PoS covered

Reading – 1b; 2c.
Speaking and listening – 2b.

# PASSPORTS

***To produce a mock version of an official document which includes personal details.***

†† *Whole-class work followed by individual work.*

🕐 *At least one hour.*

## Previous skills/knowledge needed

Children will need to understand the format and purpose of passports.

## Key background information

Passports provide basic information about people and are important documents for identification. In this activity the children make mock passports for themselves. They are given the opportunity to look at the features of a real passport and to develop their understanding of form-filling. While the passports produced will be facsimiles, they could be given practical uses. If, for example, you have arranged an educational visit for the class, the children could be asked to carry their 'passports' so that they could use them if they became lost.

*Literacy Hour:* this activity could form part of a series of Literacy Hours for the beginning of Y3 T1 (T19, T21), which would help you to get to know the children in your class. Other focuses could be on making tables and databases of information.

## Preparation

Find an example of a passport and produce an enlargement or mock-up of the page which provides details of the holder. Some of the children in your class may hold passports from other countries. If you approach parents with sensitivity, it may be possible to show examples from other parts of the world. Older passports were stamped in each country the holder visited. If you can get hold of one of these, it may provide fascinating information for the children and you could look at the passport in conjunction with an atlas.

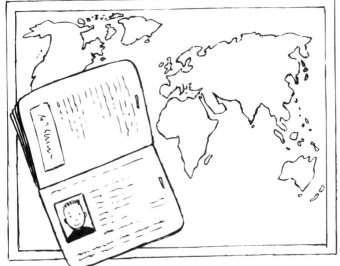

Obtain small photographs of the children (you could take a class photograph and then cut out each individual to save money).

## Resources needed

A passport, an enlarged version of the personal information page, small photographs of the children.

## What to do

*Introduction*

Talk with the children about the use of passports and ask if any of them have been through customs. Explain that under law they now need their own passports, if they are not already on their parents' documents.

Discuss the features of the passport and talk about the first page which requests in the name of the monarch that the holder be allowed 'to pass freely without let or hindrance' into other countries. Explain what this means and invite the children to suggest alternative ways in which this might be expressed in simpler, more straightforward terms.

Show the children the personal details page and then use a mock-up of an uncompleted page to fill in the details of one person in the class or of yourself.

*Individual/group work*

Ask the children to produce a personal details page for their passport and then to go on to produce a cover. You may wish to provide a standard template form for everyone to complete or you may ask the children to create them individually.

## Suggestion(s) for extension

Children could look at the layout of passports and suggest ways in which it could be improved. For example, they might research how identity cards are printed with electronic codes.

## Suggestion(s) for support

If children need help with some sections of the personal details, have the register handy so that you can confirm spellings of addresses, dates of birth and so on.

## Assessment opportunities

Look for evidence that children are able to make a simple record of information using a passport format.

## Opportunities for IT

Use the computer to create templates for passports to give a 'professional' look to them. The computer could also be used for the cover design and might incorporate the school crest if one exists. The passport information could be stored on a class database.

## Display ideas

Each child's passport may be displayed on the wall or on a table initially, but try to ensure that there are practical uses for the passports such as providing children with a means of identification on school visits.

## Other aspects of the English PoS covered

Reading – 1b.
Speaking and listening – 1a.

# CERTIFICATES

***To use the features of layout and presentation appropriate for certificates.***

†† *Whole-class work followed by individual work.*

🕐 *At least one hour.*

## Previous skills/knowledge needed

Children will need to understand the format and purpose of certificates.

## Key background information

Children receive certificates for all sorts of things, including good work, cycling proficiently, swimming and sports. In this activity they are asked to design certificates for a class display. They will look at real certificates and focus on design and layout and the way in which these features are used to enhance presentation.

*Literacy Hour:* this activity could form part of a series of Literacy Hours which focus on the presentation of written work. This could be done in Y4 T3 (W15) to help the children to use their handwriting and presentational skills effectively.

## Preparation

Make a collection of certificates, perhaps asking the children to bring in some of their own.

## Resources needed

A collection of certificates, good quality thick paper or card, draft paper, rulers, writing and drawing materials.

## What to do

*Introduction*

Begin by looking at some of the certificates from the collection and talking about why they were awarded and the ways in which they are set out. Discuss the different fonts and letter sizes and show the children how these can be achieved using the computer.

Look at some of the key words which appear on certificates and write these on the board to create a wordbank on which children may draw when producing their own certificates. The certificates could be for achievement in various fields including sport, entertainment, academic work or conduct. Key words might include: *award, awarded, certificate, certify, achieved, presented, attained* and *recognition*. Many of the words have roots which can be used as the basis for other words. For example, *achieve* and *achievement*, *recognize* and *recognition*, *present* and *presented/presentation*.

### Individual/group work
Explain to the children that they will be making their own certificates for a class display. (These can be for themselves, or they can make them in recognition of a friend's achievements.) Ask the children to plan their certificates in rough before they make final copies on good quality paper. Encourage them to use a ruler and pencil and remind them to write faintly in pencil before using indelible pens so that they ensure that words will fit onto the page.

Encourage the children to use a range of styles of writing and to vary the size of the words according to their importance.

### Suggestion(s) for extension
Some children could go on to add more detail to their certificates including a few sentences of commendation.

### Suggestion(s) for support
You may need to provide faint pencil lines to help some children with layout. Check the children's spellings before they begin to use pens.

### Assessment opportunities
Look for evidence that children are able to use a range of styles of writing and presentation to produce eye-catching certificates. Note, too, their ability to be consistent in the size and proportion of letters within words.

### Opportunities for IT
This activity lends itself to the use of desktop publishing and you may wish to have all children use this after planning by hand. Encourage the inclusion of illustrations and decoration which many computer packages feature.

### Display ideas
Make a display of some real certificates and surround them with ones that the children have made. At the centre of the display, place a certificate which has different parts labelled, for example type of award, name of recipient, awarding body, date of award.

### Other aspects of the English PoS covered
Reading – 1a.
Speaking and listening – 1a.

## HOUSE SPECIFICATIONS

***To write persuasively in a style appropriate for a specific purpose. To convey information.***

♦♦ *Whole-class work followed by individual work.*
🕐 *At least one hour.*

### Previous skills/knowledge needed
Children will need to understand the format and purpose of estate agents' house specifications brochures.

### Key background information
This activity is intended to develop children's abilities to write concisely, providing factual details about houses, and persuasively, to present the houses in an appealing way.

*Literacy Hour:* this activity could be the prelude to a series of Literacy Hours for Y6 T3 in which the theme is writing in an appropriate style for different purposes (S1, T19, T22).

### Preparation
Make a collection of house specifications and photographs of houses (both internal and external) from estate agents and display these in the classroom. (Estate agents are often happy to help with this activity by providing details of houses which have already been sold.) Suggest to the children that they bring in photographs of their own houses. Make some OHTs of pictures of houses.

### Resources needed
Estate agents' house specifications, photographs and OHTs of houses, OHP, board or flip chart, writing materials.

### What to do
*Introduction*
Show the children the display of house specifications and discuss some examples. Explain that estate agents have to provide factual information about the houses they sell and that they are not allowed to be inaccurate. However, they can write about the house in such a way that they make it sound attractive to potential buyers.

Read examples of factual writing such as the descriptions of what each room includes and then contrast these with the more persuasive writing which often appears at the beginning of the specifications. Write some of the adjectives used on the board and discuss them. You will probably find some of the following: *most appealing, attractive, picturesque, delightful, conveniently situated, much sought after, spacious, compact, easily maintained, charming, desirable.*

Now write a description of a property with the children. Try to use one for which you have internal and external photographs and enlarge these using the OHP.

*Individual/group work*

Provide the children with some internal and external photographs of houses taken from estate agents' specifications; alternatively, they could use photographs of their own houses, if they have brought them in. Explain that you would like them to produce their own brochures to advertise the houses.

Encourage them to write persuasively and to use adjectives that depict the houses favourably. Ask them to describe different features of the houses and to highlight those which are especially attractive.

**Suggestion(s) for extension**

You may be able to persuade an estate agent to look at the children's specifications and write to them or even visit them in the classroom to discuss their efforts. Try to arrange with an estate agent for the children's work to be studied and for a response to be given.

**Suggestion(s) for support**

Provide a list of useful adjectives and nouns and ask the children to use them as a starting point for their descriptions. Children who experience difficulties might be paired with more able children to produce joint work.

**Assessment opportunities**

Look for evidence that children are able to write persuasively in a style appropriate for an estate agent's brochure for a house.

**Opportunities for IT**

The brochures could be produced using a word processor. If a scanner is available, photographs could be scanned in, so that a realistic copy is produced.

**Display ideas**

Display the brochures together with some produced by estate agents.

**Other aspects of the English PoS covered**

Reading – 2c.
Speaking and listening – 2b.

# A WRITTEN ARGUMENT

*To write persuasively in a real context.*

†† *Whole-class work followed by individual and paired work.*

🕐 *At least one hour.*

**Previous skills/ knowledge needed**

Children will need to understand that writing can be persuasive and be familiar with this particular kind of text.

**Key background information**

In this activity children work with partners to conduct a debate in writing. They need to spend time marshalling their arguments and preparing in note form for their writing. They may be given the opportunity to use reference sources including newspapers.

*Literacy Hour:* this activity could be part of a series of Literacy Hours for Y6 T2 which focus on constructing effective arguments (T15, T18).

**Preparation**

Find examples of editorials from local and national papers which are forceful and which deal with issues of interest to the children.

**Resources needed**

Newspapers, reference books, paper, board or flip chart, writing materials.

**What to do**

*Introduction*

Discuss an issue which is of importance to the children with the class and ask some children for their views. Subjects might include compulsory homework for primary pupils or changes to school holidays.

Write the headings *for* and *against* at the top of two columns on the board and leave an extra column for other points. Ask the children to take turns to tell you things that support or contradict a case and write these in note form in the columns. If any points are made which are general and do not fit easily into either column, write these in the third column.

Now ask the children to choose one side of the argument and to make points at greater length, drawing upon the notes. Explain that it is important to be rational and reasonable if you are to argue effectively and that an argument need not be an angry exchange of views and should be about issues rather than personalities. You may wish to use the following idea as an example and/or as a starting point for some children's arguments.

---

**A** I think that children should be allowed to ride on buses and trains free because they are too young to drive cars.

**B** I disagree. If children were allowed to ride on buses for free, the buses would be overcrowded and older people would not be able to get on them.

**A** Most adults have cars. They could drive them instead and leave the buses for the children.

**B** I disagree. If adults all drove cars instead of travelling on buses the roads would be even more busy than they are now and the air would be even more polluted.

**A** But if children got into the habit of travelling by bus they probably would not want to drive cars when they got older and then we would have less pollution.

**B** Yes, but…

---

### Individual/group work

Ask the children to work in pairs and assign each pair an issue to debate. Each child in each pair should take an opposing view to the other. Ask the children to spend time individually jotting down arguments for and against the issue and then ask each to write a sentence which puts their case. When they have done this they should exchange papers, read each other's sentences and then respond to them before writing another sentence to support their side of the argument. Encourage them not to be dismissive of other people's views and insist that they do not refute arguments by using words like *rubbish*, *nonsense* and *stupid*.

The written argument should continue for as long as you feel children have ideas to express in a reasonable way. It is important to hold a plenary session to discuss the quality of the arguments which people put forward and to highlight the need for clarity and reasonableness. The arguments could be presented to the rest of the class, with pairs of children taking turns to read their sentences aloud.

### Suggestion(s) for extension

Some children could go on to write speeches in preparation for a class debate.

### Suggestion(s) for support

It may be appropriate for some children to begin their work by taking turns to make their points orally, with the written element limited to making brief notes.

### Assessment opportunities

Look for evidence that children are able to construct effective and persuasive arguments and can present them logically and effectively.

### Other aspects of the English PoS covered

Reading – 1c.
Speaking and listening – 2b.

---

## INTERPRETING CHARTS

*To write simple non-chronological reports from known information.*

†† *Whole-class work followed by individual work within groups.*

🕐 *At least one hour.*

---

### Previous skills/knowledge needed

Children will need to understand how information can be presented in charts and tables.

### Key background information

This activity can be linked to work done in mathematics on data handling. Children are asked to explain, in writing, the data which appears in a chart. They may go on to create their own charts and tables and write explanatory notes.

The activity provides an opportunity to explain the use of comparative and superlative adjectives such as *taller* and *tallest*, *heavier* and *heaviest* and *shorter* and *shortest*.

*Literacy Hour:* this lesson could be developed into a series of Literacy Hours for Y3 T1 in which children are required to write short non-chronological reports based upon reading charts of information (T22).

### Preparation

Make multiples copies, one for each child, of photocopiable page 104 and/or create tables of your own which are relevant to some work that the children have been doing recently. Collect some similar examples from school textbooks such as books that are part of mathematics schemes.

### Resources needed

Examples of tables and charts (see 'Preparation'), photocopiable page 104, paper, writing materials.

### What to do

*Introduction*

Look at a simple table of data with the children and ask questions which require them to find information. Use the table on photocopiable page 104 and ask questions such as:

▲ How tall is Tom?

▲ How much does Grace weigh?

▲ How long did it take Milo to run 50 metres?

When the children have clearly understood how to read the chart, ask them more interpretative questions such as:

▲ Who is taller, Naseem or Helen?

▲ Who is the fastest runner?

▲ Which child is lightest?

Discuss the use of comparative and superlative adjectives and explain that you can be the *heavier/taller/faster* and so on of two people, but that when there are more than two you become the *heaviest/tallest/fastest* and so on.

### Individual/group work

Provide the children with copies of photocopiable page 104 and ask them to write a series of statements that describe the data. Encourage them to write sentences which interpret the data, using comparative and superlative adjectives. These could include sentences such as: *Grace is shorter and lighter than Milo, but can run faster. Tom is the youngest member of the group and the slowest runner, but he is taller than Helen.*

Some groups may be asked to write simple sentences which describe single items of data. For example: *Helen is 7 years and 2 months old. Milo is 152cm tall.*

Others could be asked to write more complex sentences which include subordinate clauses and phrases. For example: *Milo, who is 10 years and 6 months old, weighs 33kg. Naseem, who is 143cm tall, can run 50 metres in 12 seconds.*

### Suggestion(s) for extension

Ask the children to create their own tables and charts using real data and to write interpretations of these, using similar techniques to those used for the photocopiable sheet.

### Suggestion(s) for support

Some children may need a set of questions to answer to help them to focus on the data. For example: how tall is Milo? How much does Helen weigh?

### Assessment opportunities

Look for evidence that children are able to write concisely and clearly, drawing upon the information provided in the tables.

### Opportunities for IT

Computer databases on children's height, weight and so on could be created and used as a source of data for this activity. These could be kept throughout the school year and could be updated as children grow.

### Display ideas

Make a display that shows the heights, weights and so on of the children in your class and update it as the children grow. Display questions alongside the table which children could answer as part of group activities for literacy or numeracy lessons.

### Other aspects of the English PoS covered

Reading – 1b.

Speaking and listening – 1a.

### Reference to photocopiable sheet

Photocopiable page 104 provides a set of alphanumeric data in the form of a table. This can be used to model the process of describing and interpreting such data in words.

| Child's name | Age | Height | Weight | Time taken to run 50 metres |
|---|---|---|---|---|
| Grace | 9Y 4M | 135cm | 31kg | 10 seconds |
| Milo | 10Y 6M | 152cm | 33kg | 11 seconds |
| Naseem | 8Y 3M | 143cm | 29kg | 12 seconds |
| Tom | 6Y 8M | 136cm | 24kg | 22 seconds |
| Helen | 7Y 2M | 129cm | 26kg | 20 seconds |

Interpreting charts

# MATCH REPORTS (1)

***To use the characteristics of report writing.***

†† *Whole-class work followed by paired or individual work.*

🕒 *At least one hour.*

## Previous skills/knowledge needed

Children will need to be aware of the ways in which match reports can be presented in newspapers.

## Key background information

This activity introduces match reports and demonstrates the importance of using lively and interesting language in order to engage the reader's interest. Match reports are readily available in newspapers and are often read by children.

*Literacy Hour:* See 'Match reports (2)'.

## Preparation

Make an enlarged copy and multiple copies of the match reports on photocopiable page 105. Find examples of match reports from newspapers.

## Resources needed

Photocopiable page 105, paper, writing materials. Newspapers containing match reports, for extension activity.

## What to do

*Introduction*

Show the children an enlarged version of the two match reports on photocopiable page 105 and read each in turn with them. Ask them which they prefer and why. Ask which report gives the better impression of what it was like to be at the match and why. You could also discuss which report the children think is most likely to be accurate and whether one of the reporters appears to be biased towards Barnsley. Discuss the use of adjectives and adverbs and the way in which attention is given to some details, such as Barnard's goal.

Explain that reporters are given limited and different amounts of space to fill with their reports and so some have to be more concise than others. The first report has about 135 words including the title, while the second has about 185. Tell the children that they have a limit of 200 words (or another figure which you think appropriate) and that they have to stick to this.

*Individual/group work*

Distribute copies of photocopiable page 105 and ask the children to work in pairs or individually to write their own versions of the match report. Encourage them to describe all the key parts of the match but to select some to develop and enhance.

If children exceed the word limit, ask them to read through their reports and edit them to eliminate any unnecessary words such as *got*. You may wish to show them an example of unnecessarily wordy text to explain this point: *Barnsley had got five goals by the time the first 37 minutes of the match had gone.*

could be condensed to: *Barnsley had five goals in the first 37 minutes.*

Emphasize that, while they should be concise, the children should also look for ways to embellish their writing by using adverbs and adjectives to create a picture of the match for their readers.

## Suggestion(s) for extension

Children who finish their work early and complete the editing and revising process could be asked to look at a selection of match reports from newspapers and comment on them, before editing and revising them.

## Suggestion(s) for support

Some children may need to work with an adult to list key events and then write simple sentences to describe each one. Adverbs and adjectives could then be added as part of a shared writing session.

## Assessment opportunities

Look for evidence that children are able to select information and present it in a journalistic style.

## Opportunities for IT

Some children could produce their reports on a word processor. Children who have completed work could use the Internet, if this is available, to find and read match reports.

## Display ideas

Display newspaper match reports together with the children's work. Pictures should be interspersed with the writing.

## Other aspects of the English PoS covered
Reading – 2c.
Speaking and listening – 2b.

## Reference to photocopiable sheet
Photocopiable page 105 shows two reports of the same football match – one dry and factual, the other vivid and dramatic. The children can contrast these reports and write their own version of events.

# MATCH REPORTS (2)

*To use the characteristics of report writing.*

†† *Individuals or pairs writing reports.*
🕐 *One to one and a half hours.*

## Previous skills/knowledge needed
This activity follows on from the previous activity 'Match reports (1)', which it would be helpful if the children have completed. They will need to have discussed some of the attributes of successful report writing, such as the use of adjectives and adverbs, brevity and conciseness.

## Key background information
This activity should help children to develop their ability to write reports and should increase their awareness of the qualities of successful report writing.

*Literacy Hour:* this activity could take place over a series of Literacy Hours with a different focus in each. For example, for a series of five Literacy Hours for Y6 in Term 1, the focus might be:

▲ Hour 1: commenting on style in reports (T12)
▲ Hour 2: planning in note form (revision)
▲ Hour 3: writing reports, looking at ways of connecting points (S4, S5)
▲ Hour 4: awareness of the interest of the reader (T15)
▲ Hour 5: using journalistic style (T16).

## Preparation
Gather together a collection of match reports from newspapers and display them. Take one example and enlarge it so that you can discuss it with the children. Make a video recording of brief highlights of a sports event.

## Resources needed
Match reports, a video recording of brief highlights of a sports event, board or flip chart, draft paper, writing materials.

## What to do
*Introduction*
Show the children the example of a match report and discuss the way in which it is set out. Talk about the headline and other information such as the match score and the journalist's name. Some reports also include lists of teams and gradings of players' performances.

Explain that you are going to show the children some brief highlights of a match and ask them to write reports. Show the video recording and then ask the children to tell you what the key events were. Write these on the board as the children suggest them and then ask them to help you to number the events chronologically. Tell the children that journalists need to consider the following when writing match reports:
▲ interesting the reader
▲ providing details of key events
▲ keeping reports within specified word limits
▲ describing events in such a way that the excitement of the match is conveyed to the reader.

*Individual/group work*
Show the video again, but this time show only one key event at a time, and then ask the children to make rough notes on what happened in each section.

When the children have seen all of the video, ask them to use their notes as the basis for a match report. You may wish to specify a word limit to encourage them to be concise. During the writing period, stop the children occasionally to read aloud examples of good descriptions and to encourage the use of adjectives and adverbs to enliven the reports. You may also wish to discuss the use of synonyms. For example, if the report is on a soccer match the children may use different ways of describing the ball being kicked into the goal. Find some examples in the collection of reports that you have displayed. These might include: *slotted the ball home, crashed the ball into the net, thumped home a shot, smashed in an unstoppable shot, slammed the ball past the keeper.*

Play the whole section of video again and pause occasionally to ask some children to read aloud their descriptions of particular parts of the match.

### Suggestion(s) for extension

Ask the children to write reports on school matches. These could be done in note form and then written up in class. Children who are injured and unable to take part in PE lessons might produce reports on small-sided games.

### Suggestion(s) for support

This activity could be done by two or three children working together, with one acting as a scribe and including the others' ideas as well as his or her own. A word list of verbs, adverbs and adjectives could be provided through a brainstorming session and could be available to the whole class for support.

### Assessment opportunities

Look for evidence that children are able to adopt a concise, journalistic style which engages and interests readers.

### Opportunities for IT

If the school has access to the Internet, it will be possible to find websites for sports clubs. These include brief match reports as well as news about the team. Encourage the children to explore these.

The match reports could be published using a newspaper desktop publishing program, with photographs incorporated.

### Display ideas

Produce a sports paper that contains reports on different matches or display a selection of reports on the match that the class first wrote about, together with action photographs and examples of the children's reports.

### Other aspects of the English PoS covered

Reading – 2c.
Speaking and listening – 2b.

## EXCUSE NOTES

***To write an explanation. To parody a persuasive statement.***

†† *Individuals or pairs devising absence excuses and writing letters of explanation.*

🕐 *One hour.*

### Key background information

This activity offers children the opportunity to be creative in their writing of excuses.

*Literacy Hour:* this activity could form part of a series of Literacy Hours for Y3 T3 (T20) which focus on writing letters, notes and messages, or for Y5 T2 with an emphasis upon explanatory texts (T22).

### Preparation

Devise some examples of excuse notes, writing them on a large sheet of paper. For example: *Dear Mrs Jones, I am sorry that Kevin has not done his homework. He was going to do it but the dog ate his exercise book.* If you have any examples of interesting excuse notes which could be used anonymously, you could enlarge these after concealing the names.

### Resources needed

Examples of excuse notes (see 'Preparation'), paper, board or flip chart, writing materials.

### What to do

*Introduction*

Show the children some examples of notes which offer strange excuses for absence or failure to complete work. Ask them if they would believe the writers if they were the teacher who received them. What evidence might lead them to suspect that the notes might not be authentic?

Ask the children to think of some unusual excuses and write some of their ideas on the board in preparation for shared writing.

Write a sample excuse note with the children's help. Discuss the structure of the note and features such as using *Yours sincerely* when writing to someone who is named, and *Yours faithfully* when the salutation is *Dear Sir* or *Dear Madam.* Talk about the importance of brevity and being imaginative in the excuses that are used.

*Individual/group work*

Provide each pair of children with a list of situations which might require an excuse note (see below) and ask them to write brief excuse notes for each circumstance. Encourage them to be creative and to think of unusual and interesting excuses. Emphasize that you are looking for interesting and, if possible, amusing excuses. The different circumstances could be as follows:

▲ not wearing school uniform when you are expected to

Dear Mr. Bennett,
I have been
abducted by aliens

▲ not being able to do games
▲ being late for school
▲ not learning spellings
▲ being away from school
▲ losing a book which belongs to school.

Stop the class occasionally to share ideas and to write on the board any words which are causing problems for several children.

## Suggestion(s) for extension

Give the children further circumstances to write excuses for at greater length. These might include more complex situations such as turning up at school wearing a pink dress, as Bill does in Anne Fine's *Bill's New Frock* (Mammoth), or being found in possession of a large number of sleepy pheasants, as Danny and his father are in Roald Dahl's *Danny the Champion of the World* (Puffin).

## Suggestion(s) for support

Some children may need to work under the guidance of an adult who could help them to think of ideas and who could provide a wordbank for them to draw upon. This might include: *unable, accident, apologize, absent, sincerely* and *faithfully*.

## Assessment opportunities

Look for evidence that children are able to write from someone else's point of view to retell an incident in the form of a letter.

## Opportunities for IT

Key in the list of different circumstances, and ask the children to write an excuse in response to each one, at the computer. When several children have done this, there will be a set of excuse notes for each circumstance, which can then be compared.

## Display ideas

Display the children's excuse notes together with the list of different situations.

## Other aspects of the English PoS covered

Reading – 2c.
Speaking and listening – 1a.

# MOTTOES

*To understand the nature of mottoes and to devise their own.*

†† *Whole-class work followed by paired work.*

🕒 *Up to one hour.*

## Key background information

Many organizations have mottoes which appear on badges and crests. The mottoes are intended to give an impression of the ethos of the organizations. Some are in Latin but most which appear in Britain are in English. For example: *Lend a hand* – Brownie Guides; *Do your best* – Cub Scouts; *Be prepared* – Scouts and Guides; *Who dares wins* – SAS.

This activity offers children the chance to invent mottoes for well-known organizations and emphasizes the need for brevity and skilful use of words.

## Preparation

Find examples of badges and crests with mottoes. These could include mottoes in languages other than English, providing you are able to translate them. In advance of the lesson you could ask children to look for badges and crests at home and bring in examples.

## Resources needed

Examples of mottoes, paper, board or flip chart, writing materials.

## What to do

*Introduction*

Show the children some examples of mottoes and ask them if they know of any others. Talk about the way in which an idea can be given about the aims, beliefs or self-image of an organization using very few words.

Choose organizations which are well-known to the children and ask for suggestions for mottoes. Write the children's suggestions on the board and then invite them to modify and improve them.

*Individual/group work*

Ask the children to work in pairs to write mottoes for different organizations. (The designing of the crests could take place during an art or design lesson.)

Encourage the children to be concise and to consider the characteristics of the organizations when choosing their words. Stop the class occasionally to draw attention to good ideas and to invite the children to suggest ideas for those who are struggling to think of any.

## Suggestion(s) for extension

Invite the children to suggest mottoes for the school, if it does not already have one. They could go on to design a crest which could be displayed in the entrance to the school.

## Suggestion(s) for support
Some children may find it difficult to think of mottoes. Work with a small group and use their ideas to create a selection of mottoes for different institutions, before asking them to work in pairs to create their own.

## Assessment opportunities
Look for signs that children are able to use their growing vocabularies to produce concise and pithy mottoes.

## Opportunities for IT
Crests could be designed using a computer and then mottoes could be added in an appropriately attractive font.

## Display ideas
Display examples of crests and mottoes together with the children's work. If a crest has been designed for the class, you could display it on the door to the classroom.

## Other aspects of the English PoS covered
Reading – 1c.
Speaking and listening – 3b.

# A CLASS QUIZ

*To understand how to phrase and punctuate questions.*

†† *Whole-class work followed by pairs preparing questions based upon texts that are well known to the class.*

🕐 *One hour.*

## Key background information
This activity is intended both to encourage children to look closely at books and other sources of information in the classroom and to phrase questions accurately.

*Literacy Hour:* this activity could be part of a series of Literacy Hours for Y3 T1 which focus on reading comprehension (T18), recording information (T21) and exploring sentence construction and punctuation (S6).

## Preparation
In advance of the lesson, ask the children to make up at least one question related to books and other texts that most of the class will know. The texts could be ones which the children have read themselves or had read to them, and they could include reference books such as atlases, dictionaries, encyclopaedias and thesauruses, as well as CD-ROMs.

## Resources needed
A collection of texts which are well known to the children, board or flip chart, paper, writing materials.

## What to do
*Introduction*
Ask the children for some examples of questions that they prepared in advance. Write some of these on the board and ask if anyone knows the answers. Discuss the ways in which the questions are phrased and ask for suggestions as to how they might be improved. Discuss the features of questions such as capital letters to begin sentences and question marks to end them. Talk, too, about some of the words which appear in questions such as *who, what, which, why* and *when.*

*Individual/group work*
Ask the children to work in pairs to formulate and write questions related to texts that the rest of the class know well. Encourage them to check the answers to their questions and to note the page or source on which the information which is needed to answer them appears. Stop the class occasionally to discuss progress and to remind the children about correct punctuation for questions.

## Suggestion(s) for extension
Some children could act as 'specialist question setters' to formulate a series of questions on one subject for classmates, who could then take part in a 'Mastermind quiz' competition.

## Suggestion(s) for support
Children with limited experience of extended reading could be helped to write questions based upon texts which are read to them by an adult or by the teacher.

## Assessment opportunities
Look for evidence that children are able to punctuate and phrase questions successfully. Are the answers to their questions identifiable?

## Opportunities for IT
Let the children compile their questions using the computer – a database of questions and answers could be devised. Children could make use of CD-ROMs as a source of information.

## Display ideas

Display the questions that the children produce next to the books and other sources to which they refer, and use the display as a focus for group work during Literacy Hours.

## Other aspects of the English PoS covered

Reading – 2b.
Speaking and listening – 2b.

## LETTER TO A COUNCILLOR

***To write a formal, persuasive letter for a real purpose.***

†† *Whole-class work followed by individual work.*

🕐 *At least one hour.*

## Key background information

This activity is intended to encourage children to marshal their ideas and edit and present points of view in the form of formal letters. It is important that the audiences for the children's letters are real and that there is a likelihood that they will receive a reply.

*Literacy Hour:* this activity could be part of a series of Literacy Hours for Y5 T3 (T17) which focus on writing letters for real purposes.

## Preparation

Make a collection of formal letters which argue a point of view. These could be letters written to newspapers or they could be copies of ones written by friends and colleagues. Consider some possible topics for the children's own letters. Make copies of photocopiable page 106, one for each child.

Read some of the sample formal letters to the children and discuss, in simple terms, the points of view that are being put forward.

## Resources needed

Examples of formal letters, photocopiable page 106, board or flip chart, paper, writing materials.

## What to do

*Introduction*

Distribute copies of photocopiable page 106 and read the letter with the children. Ask them to comment on its quality. Is it well written and has the author expressed her ideas clearly?

> Dear Sir,
> I am writing to tell you about the high speed of cars in our village. Something must be done about it

Ask the children to tell you the main points of the letter, and make a list of these on the board. Discuss the layout of the letter and talk about the conventions of formal letter writing such as:

▲ including the address of the recipient as well as the sender

▲ writing the date

▲ introducing the subject in the first paragraph

▲ using *Yours sincerely* if you write the recipient's name after *Dear* and *Yours faithfully* if you write *Dear Sir, Dear Madam* and so on.

You will also need to discuss the kinds of phrases which can be used to express strong feelings in writing. These might include: *absolutely disgraceful, totally unacceptable, quite appalling.* However, you should explain to children that overuse of such language can be counter-productive. Stress the importance of putting their views in a calm and reasonable way and suggest that they use emotive phrases sparingly.

Discuss possible topics for letters for the children to write and with the children's help, make a list of words which may be useful. It is important to spend time discussing whom the recipients of the letters will be, as this may affect the way in which they are written.

*Individual/group work*

Ask the children to plan their letters in note form and to look at their notes and organize them, so that their letters will be well-structured and coherent.

Encourage them to present their views persuasively, but emphasize the need to be rational, reasonable and polite. It may be a good idea to ask them to make at least three important points in their letters.

Stress that it is very important that letters be well presented and well written if they are to be taken seriously by their recipients.

You could invite a local councillor into the classroom and ask him or her to answer some of the children's questions orally.

## Suggestion(s) for extension

The children could go on to formulate questions that they would like to ask the recipients of the letters in a face-to-face discussion.

## Suggestion(s) for support

Some children could work with more able partners to compose joint letters to which they contribute ideas.

## Assessment opportunities

Look for evidence that children are able to construct an argument in note form and can draft and present a point of view.

## Opportunities for IT

Encourage some children to draft, edit and revise their letters using the word processor.

## Display ideas

Ideally, the letters will be sent to a councillor or member of parliament and will receive a reply. Make photocopies of the letters to display in the classroom.

## Other aspects of the English PoS covered

Reading – 2c.
Speaking and listening – 2b.

## Reference to photocopiable sheet

Photocopiable page 106 shows an example of a formal letter written to persuade an individual. The children can use this as a model for their own similar letters.

# BOOK ADVERTISEMENTS

***To write persuasively using features of presentation appropriate for advertisements.***

†† *Individuals or pairs producing advertisements for books which they have read.*

🕐 *At least one hour.*

## Key background information

This activity is intended to encourage children to look at the design of printed advertisements and to produce their own adverts for books that they have enjoyed. The activity may be extended to include oral presentations and could form part of a school book week.

*Literacy Hour:* this activity could be part of a series of Literacy Hours for Y4 T3 which concentrate on advertisements (T25) and handwriting skills (W15). These lessons could focus on presentation of information and include work on linguistic devices such as puns, jingles, alliteration and invented words (T19).

## Preparation

In advance of the lesson, ask children to find in school or bring from home their favourite books. Have a selection of books which you or your colleagues have read to the children in the past. Produce an advertisement for a favourite book of your own or find examples from newspapers and magazines. Find some exciting excerpts from books which the children know well.

## Resources needed

Books, book excerpts and book advertisements (see 'Preparation'), chalkboard/whiteboard, paper, writing and drawing materials.

## What to do

*Introduction*

Show the children samples of advertisements for books and discuss their presentation. Ask them about the text that has been used and discuss any unfamiliar words. Ask questions such as:

▲ What catches your eye when you look at the adverts?

▲ Which are the key words?

▲ Which aspects of the adverts make you feel you would (or would not) like to read the books?

▲ Who do you think the adverts are aimed at?

Invite some children to tell the class about their favourite books and encourage them to think about excerpts which could be used to attract readers.

Work with the children to model a draft advertisement for a book. (This is best done on a chalkboard or whiteboard so that ideas can be erased and changed easily.) Encourage them to make suggestions about the way in which the advertisement should be presented. Talk about key words and ask them to offer ideas about which words should be produced in large and small print. Discuss the importance of making adverts eye-catching and appealing to readers.

*Individual/group work*

Ask the children to produce their own advertisements for their favourite books. Emphasize the importance of attracting readers through interesting presentation and carefully selected extracts from the text.

Encourage them to plan their work out carefully to ensure that words will fit in the right places. This could be done by using faint pencil at the drafting stage. Stop the class occasionally to share good ideas and to discuss any problems.

When the children feel confident that they have produced successful draft advertisements, work with them to check spellings and layout before they go on to use felt-tipped pens for their final pieces of work.

## Suggestion(s) for extension

Suggest that the children go on to write and produce oral advertisements which could be presented to the rest of the class or to the school.

## Suggestion(s) for support

Children with limited reading skills may be encouraged to work with more capable partners. Adult help may be needed to help them to find exciting extracts from books which they have had read to them.

## Assessment opportunities

Look for evidence that children are able to design an advertisement using the features that they have seen in published adverts.

## Opportunities for IT

There are many design packages which could be used to produce advertisements. Children might use a scanner to incorporate pictures into their adverts.

## Display ideas

Display the children's advertisements along with the books which they advertise, in order to encourage them to look at the books.

## Other aspects of the English PoS covered

Reading – 2c.
Speaking and listening – 2a.

## THE TOWN (1)

*To write short autobiographies in role.*

†† *Individuals writing autobiographies of invented characters.*

⏱ *At least one hour.*

## Previous skills/knowledge needed

Children will need to understand what is meant by an autobiography and a biography. They should understand that they will be writing autobiographically, but in role.

## Key background information

This activity is the first in a series of activities which involve cross-curricular work, but with English at its core. The activities revolve around a town or village created with the children. Maps and scale models can be used to provide an image of the town, in addition to photocopiable page 107. The written work may involve the children in writing directions, letters, biographies and descriptions. There could also be opportunities for creating a newspaper and for producing posters.

The first lesson could be linked to work on curriculum vitae and involves autobiographical writing in role.

*Literacy Hour:* this activity, together with the three following activities on 'The town', could form part of a series of lessons across the curriculum which include Literacy Hours for Y6 in T1. They could be used as starting points for extended work, and they could also be linked to other work in language study, such as addressing an envelope, and in imaginative writing, such as story writing.

## Preparation

Make an enlarged copy of photocopiable page 107. Photocopy page 108 (preferably onto card) and cut it into individual sections to make fictitious name cards for the children showing the roles they will play within the town. Decide on a role that you will allocate to yourself.

## Resources needed

Photocopiable pages 107 and 108, card (optional), paper, board or flip chart, writing materials. A set of cards with information about characters, for support activity.

## What to do

*Introduction*

Show the children the plan of the imaginary town on an enlarged copy of photocopiable page 107 and discuss the names of different parts of it. Explain that each child or pair of children will have fictitious identities within the town. They may, for instance, be householders, but they will also have a role to play within the town, so they could be shopkeepers, police, doctors and so on. Allocate different roles to the children, and provide them with their name cards made from a copy of photocopiable page 108.

When the children have been given their identities within the town, ask them to invent biographies for themselves. Work through a sample autobiography for your own character and ask the children to help you. Include the names of your immediate family, your age (fictitious!), your occupation, your hobbies and interests and any other information that you care to choose. Write all the information on the board.

### Individual/group work

Ask the children to use the format of the sample autobiography to invent details about their own characters. Encourage them to invent hobbies and interests as well as age, date, place of birth and so on. Where children have characters who are related, ask them to get together to agree on some of the family details. Remind them that their autobiographies should be written in the first person in role.

Stop the class occasionally to discuss the autobiographies and read some examples aloud.

### Suggestion(s) for extension

The children could go on to write brief biographies of other members of their characters' families or of other local personalities.

### Suggestion(s) for support

If some children are struggling to think of different facets of their invented characters, allow them to draw on ideas from cards which provide character traits or snippets of information. These could include such things as: *Mr Morton plays for the town football team. Mrs Robson won a prize for her cooking. Mr Wilson is captain of the tennis team. Revd. Morris is a keen bird-watcher.* The children can then use these basic facts to add further details about their characters.

### Assessment opportunities

Look for evidence that children are able to write autobiographies in role – is there consistency in the characterization and is there enough attention to detail?

### Opportunities for IT

Ask some children to produce a database using the information provided in the biographies. This could be used to create a parish register or electoral role, as well as being a source of reference throughout the project.

### Display ideas

As part of art, design & technology or geography work, ask the children to draw pictures, make models and devise maps of the town, based on photocopiable page 107.

### Other aspects of the English PoS covered

Reading – 1b.
Speaking and listening – 1d (drama).

### Reference to photocopiable sheets

Photocopiable page 107 is a simple plan of an imaginary town, which provides a context for the activity and helps the children to focus on the identities that they assume when writing their autobiographies in role. Photocopiable page 108 provides fictitious name cards which are allocated to the children, in order for them to assume their assorted roles within the town.

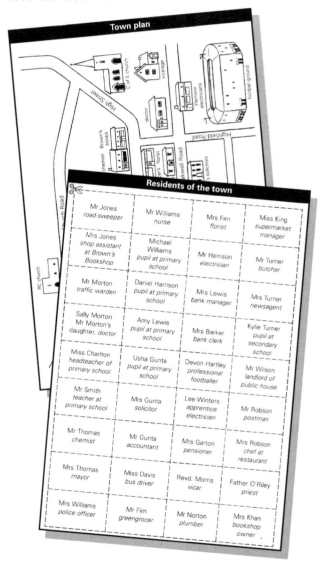

# THE TOWN (2)

*To write a letter in role.*

†† *Individuals, pairs and groups.*

🕒 *At least one hour.*

## Previous skills/knowledge needed

Children should understand how letters should be set out and should be aware of differences between formal and informal letters.

## Key background information

This activity, the second in the series, allows characters within the town to communicate with each other. The children use their completed autobiographies as the basis for letters to other townspeople, who in turn write back to them.

## Preparation

Before the activity, do some work with the children on addresses and addressing an envelope. Ask the children to decide upon street names and addresses for their invented characters. Prepare a set of cards (one per child) with the names and the children's chosen addresses of the town residents (perhaps using a database printout). Write an example of an informal (personal) letter and make an enlarged photocopy of it.

## Resources needed

Cards with the names and addresses of town residents (see 'Preparation'), an enlarged copy of an informal letter, the children's autobiographies from the previous activity, paper, writing materials.

## What to do

*Introduction*

Explain that you are going to give a card with the name and address of a town resident to each child, and that the children will then write a letter in role to the person whose

name is on the card. When you are distributing the cards, make sure that you avoid having characters writing to close family members or to themselves!

Discuss the format of informal letters and provide an enlarged example.

*Individual/group work*

Ask the children to use the autobiographies that they wrote in the previous activity, 'The town (1)', as a starting point for their letters. When they have been assigned a person to write to, ask them to read that person's autobiography so that they know something about him or her.

Explain that they are writing for a purpose and that the letters should be informal. They could begin by thanking the person for a gift or inviting them to visit. Encourage the children to be imaginative in their choice of material and tell them that, providing the information they give does not contradict what is in their autobiographies, they have licence to invent characters and situations for themselves.

## Suggestion(s) for extension

The lesson could be developed into a hot-seating activity, with some children answering questions from the rest of the class in role.

## Suggestion(s) for support

Some children may need the help of an adult to compose a letter. If necessary, help them to begin their letters by acting as a scribe. Provide them with a list of useful words such as: *Dear, sincerely, confirm, considerably, arrangements, visit, delighted.*

## Assessment opportunities

Look for evidence that children are able to write letters in role using the conventions of informal letter writing.

## Opportunities for IT

Some children could compose letters using the word processor. For those children who experience difficulties in writing at length, you could provide a template letter with key phrases and spaces for the children to include the personal details of their characters.

Subsequent to the activity, the databases could be updated to include any new information that characters have provided.

## Display ideas

Ask the children to address envelopes to the people to whom they are writing, and make a postbox for them to post them in. They could be delivered by Mr Robson, the postman (see photocopiable page 108)!

## Other aspects of the English PoS covered

Reading – 1c.

Speaking and listening – 1a.

# THE TOWN (3)

***To use sequential text to write directions.***

†† *Individuals, pairs and groups writing directions.*

🕐 *One hour.*

## Previous skills/knowledge needed

Children should understand ways in which directions can be given using key terms such as *first left, second right* and *straight on*.

## Key background information

This activity enables the children to get to know their fictitious town better, and involves them in writing directions for travelling from one part of the town to another.

## Preparation

Make a set of cards which have the names of each building in the town (see photocopiable page 107). The children could make these in advance. Make an enlarged copy of photocopiable page 107, or make multiple copies so that the children can look at the plan of the town in pairs.

## Resources needed

Cards with names of buildings within the town (see 'Preparation'), photocopiable page 107, paper, writing materials.

## What to do

### Introduction

Show the children the cards that have the names of different buildings in the town. Look at the plan of the town together and then invite different children, one at a time, to come out and take two cards. They should then give directions for the journey between the two buildings. Encourage the children to describe the journey, looking at the plan but without pointing to it, and ask them to use words such as *left, right, straight on, opposite* and phrases such as *second on the left* and *first right* to make their directions specific and clear. Talk about the use of words which indicate a sequence of directions such as *first, then, next* and *finally,* and encourage the children to use these orally.

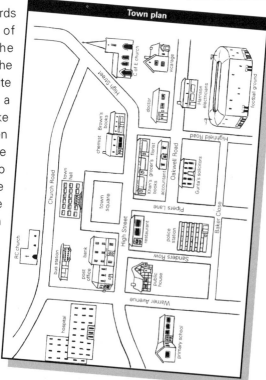

Town plan

## Individual/group work

Provide each group of children with some cards and ask them to take two each and to write directions for journeys between the places indicated. Ask them to use words which indicate a sequence (*first, next, finally* and so on) to begin their sentences. Encourage the children to try out their directions on each other, using the town plan.

When the children have written one set of directions, they may take further cards and repeat the exercise.

## Suggestion(s) for extension

You could provide extra cards which indicate how a journey is to be made, since this may affect the routes taken. These could include: *on foot, on a bicycle, by bus, by car.*

## Suggestion(s) for support

Some children may need to work with more able partners who can act as scribes to help them to record their directions. Alternatively, provide them with a file to work on at the computer which has words that can be used when writing a sequence. For example, the beginning of each line could start with a different word such as *First... Next... After that... Finally...*

## Assessment opportunities

Look for evidence that children are able to write directions accurately using words which indicate a sequence.

## Opportunities for IT

Some children could use the word processor to produce their directions. (Also, see 'Suggestion(s) for support'.)

## Display ideas

Display the children's directions next to an enlarged copy of the town plan on photocopiable page 107. Place the set of names of buildings next to the plan, and encourage the children to use them to work out routes orally and in writing when they have completed other work. They could do this by taking turns to draw two cards at random.

## Other aspects of the English PoS covered

Reading – 1c.
Speaking and listening – 1a.

## Reference to photocopiable sheet

The children refer to photocopiable page 107 when they give directions to show the route from one building to another within the town.

# THE TOWN (4)

***To use a journalistic style.***

†† *Individuals, pairs and groups.*

🕑 *One to two hours.*

## Previous skills/knowledge needed

Children should have experienced journalistic writing before and should be aware of terms such as *headline, article* and *report.*

## Key background information

In this activity children are asked to write as journalists about parts of their town and to describe important features. You may wish to link the activity to an art or design lesson in which drawings or models are produced.

## Preparation

Find some examples of local newspapers and cut out and enlarge selected articles and reports. You could use the reports from the activity 'Match reports (1)' (see photocopiable page 105) as examples too.

## Resources needed

Examples of local newspaper reports and articles, board or flip chart, paper, writing materials.

## What to do

*Introduction*

Read some of the newspaper articles and reports with the children, and discuss their content and style.

Ask the children to suggest some things which could happen in the town which might be worth reporting in its local paper. Make a note of their suggestions on the board.

*Individual/group work*

Explain that the children are going to be reporters, and that their reports will be put together to create a local paper for their imaginary town. Help the children to decide what their reports are going to be about, referring to the list on the board. You will need to ensure that there is a diversity of news, and that children do not decide to 'kill characters off'! Ask the children to write their reports, including as much information as they can but making the text concise.

NB It may be a good idea to leave the sports page of the newspaper until the news has been reported, in order to avoid having too many match reports from the football fans in the class.

## Suggestion(s) for extension

When children have completed one report, ask them to write other pieces for parts of the newspaper which have yet to be written. These could include: letters to the editor; editorials; television reviews; weather forecasts; advertisements for local businesses.

## Suggestion(s) for support

Children who experience problems could be helped by working with partners or with an adult. Key questions could be provided to give the children more confidence about what the content of their report should include. For example, if they are writing about an accident that has happened in the town: *Where did the accident happen? When? How many people were involved? Were there any eyewitnesses?* and so on.

## Assessment opportunities

Look for evidence that children are able to adopt a journalistic style.

## Opportunities for IT

Ask the children to take turns to use a desktop publishing package to produce their articles and reports on the computer, so that a professional looking newspaper may be produced. Some of the children who have completed their work could act as editors.

## Display ideas

Make multiple copies of the town newspaper. Display pages on the wall for use as a starting point for future lessons.

## Other aspects of the English PoS covered

Reading – 1b.

Speaking and listening – 1a.

# Language study

This chapter provides activities which should encourage children to develop their understanding of the way in which their language is structured, and ways in which it can be used.

Throughout the activities, there is an emphasis on the use of correct terminology and the development of a vocabulary which may be used when discussing writing.

Some of the activities involve children doing short exercises which are intended to confirm their understanding of concepts. However, such exercises, while useful, should not be allowed to stand alone and should be part of a range of activities which children undertake. Opportunities should be sought to develop understanding of language through creative work as well as through exercises, and there should also be a strong emphasis upon oral work, with extensive class and group discussions being a feature of lessons.

A starting point for any exploration of grammar should be reading, and opportunities should be sought for providing examples of language usage within texts which are accessible to children, wherever possible.

The advent of prescribed curricula for English has rightly placed considerable emphasis upon the development of knowledge about language. Access to such knowledge provides children and teachers with a means of exploring language together and understanding why mistakes are sometimes made. It also helps young writers to become more confident and adventurous in their writing.

## VOCABULARY EXTENSION (1)

***To identify adverbs and insert them in a passage of prose.***

**††** *Whole-class work followed by paired work.*

🕐 *At least one hour.*

### Previous skills/knowledge needed
The children will need to understand that adverbs can be used to modify verbs.

### Key background information
In this activity the children are shown how adverbs can be used to enhance writing, and how to make it clear to the reader how certain things within the context of a sentence are done. Although the aim is to encourage them to make greater use of adverbs, they should also realize that it is not necessary to use an adverb every time they use a verb.

*Literacy Hour:* this activity could be developed into a series of Literacy Hours for Y4 T1 as follows:
▲ Hour 1: sentence-level focus on the use of adverbs (S4)
▲ Hour 2: planning a story which continues from the opening paragraph of 'The Escape' (T9 and 10)
▲ Hour 3: continuing the story and focusing on the use of paragraphs (T10)
▲ Hour 4: sentence-level grammatical awareness work looking more closely at the use of adverbs (S4).

### Preparation
Find some examples of effective uses of adverbs from a story which is currently being read to the children. Make enough copies of photocopiable page 109 for at least one between two children, and then cut the sheets in half to separate the first and second versions of the story.

### Resources needed
Photocopiable page 109, writing materials.

### What to do
*Introduction*
Give each pair of children a copy of the top half of photocopiable page 109. Read this version of 'The escape' which has no adverbs. Ask the children if they think the text sounds like a potentially exciting story. Do they think they could make it more exciting by improving the descriptions? Explain the term *adverb*. Draw from them the idea that adverbs can help the reader by showing how things are done.

In order to reinforce the use of adverbs, ask the children to take turns to perform simple tasks, with the rest of the class providing adverbs to describe how the children performed them. For example, they could walk, hop, smile, laugh, jump or write, and do each *slowly, quickly, carefully* and so on.

### Individual/group work
Ask the children to work together in pairs to add adverbs, where appropriate, to the text in the first version of 'The escape'. They need not rewrite, but could simply insert a caret in the place where they would like to place an adverb and then write the word above the line. The text is double-spaced to make this possible.

> quickly
> I ran∧ down the road.

Emphasize that they should concentrate only on those verbs that they think would benefit most from some additional description, and that it is not necessary to use an adverb for every verb.

An alternative approach to this activity would be for you to place carets in the places where there are adverbs in the second version of the text and to ask the children to place their own adverbs in the same places. They could go on to look at the text critically, perhaps deleting some of the adverbs which they feel are unnecessary.

### Suggestion(s) for extension
Invite the children to write their own introductory paragraphs for the story, using their own verbs, adverbs and adjectives.

### Suggestion(s) for support
Some children may benefit from being given a list of possible adverbs which they could choose from to insert into the story.

### Assessment opportunities
Look for evidence that the children understand the impact adverbs can have on sentences. Ask them to identify adverbs in their writing and that of others, and note their ability to do so accurately.

### Opportunities for IT
Ask the children to revise the text on the photocopiable sheet, producing their own versions which incorporate adverbs. Encourage them to use the spellchecker to ensure that they have spelled their adverbs correctly.

### Display ideas
Make a display of common verbs, accompanied by examples of adverbs which could be used with them, and sentences that contain each verb–adverb pair. The children could draw illustrations to be placed around the text.

### Other aspects of the English PoS covered
Speaking and listening – 3b.
Reading – 2b.

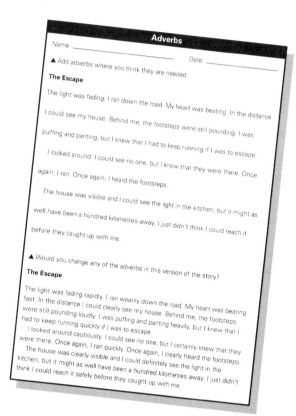

### Reference to photocopiable sheet
Photocopiable page 109 shows two versions of the same opening of a story. The first version contains no adverbs, and is double-spaced for revision; the second has some adverbs added, and is intended for reading and comment.

# VOCABULARY EXTENSION (2)

*To identify adjectives and insert them in a passage of prose.*

†† *Whole-class work followed by paired work.*

⏱ *At least one hour.*

## Previous skills/knowledge needed

The children will need to understand that adjectives can be used to modify nouns.

## Key background information

In this activity the children are presented with a passage in which rather bland adjectives have been used. They are asked to think about ways in which the text could be enlivened by the use of more interesting adjectives which enable the reader to gain a clearer picture of the scene.

*Literacy Hour:* this activity could be used for a series of Literacy Hours for Y3 in Term 2, with a focus on the use of adjectives. The activities could include: finding adjectives within their own reading books (S3); writing simple adjective/noun poems (T11); writing character portraits (T8).

## Preparation

Make a list of adjectives which appear in a story which you have recently read to the children. Make one copy of photocopiable page 110 for each pair of children, and an enlarged copy for whole-class work.

## Resources needed

Photocopiable page 110, writing materials.

## What to do

### Introduction

Read the passage from the enlarged copy with the children, and then cover it and ask them to tell you about it. Ask some children to describe the scene and encourage them to use adjectives to do so. Help the children to understand the term *adjective*, and to be able to use it appropriately, by asking them to think of adjectives which describe different items in the classroom. Ask, 'Who can think of an adjective to describe…?'

Once the children have a clear idea of what an adjective is, ask them to look at the passage again and to identify the adjectives as they read the text with you. Ask them if they can suggest alternative adjectives to those in the text, so that they can make it more interesting and 'paint a better picture' with words. Examples in the passage, such as 'the sun was hot' and 'the wet sea', could be good starting points for children to produce more interesting adjectives.

### Individual/group work

Provide the children with copies of the text (photocopiable page 110) and ask them to work in pairs to substitute their own adjectives for those in the passage whenever they feel that they could improve it. (Or they can choose from the selection in the box – see 'Suggestion(s) for support'.) They should write their words above the text, inserting a caret (see page 63). They may wish to add extra adjectives so that some nouns are described by two or more adjectives and some, which were not previously described, acquire adjectives. Explain to the children that the overuse of adjectives can spoil writing, and that they should consider whether it is necessary to use an adjective to describe every noun.

## Suggestion(s) for extension

The children could go on to write further text which includes descriptions of the beach and the children playing. Encourage them to be adventurous in their use of adjectives.

## Suggestion(s) for support

Rather than expecting the children to provide their own adjectives, let them choose from the list of possible adjectives provided in the box on the photocopiable sheet. You may need to work with some groups to model the process and to produce a collective revised version of the text.

## Assessment opportunities

Look for examples of children using adjectives appropriately, and make a note of any children who find it difficult to think of many adjectives. You may need to follow the activity by providing some opportunities for vocabulary extension work, using published books.

## Opportunities for IT

Present the text on the photocopiable sheet as a file on the word processor, so that the children can highlight the words and use 'cut' and 'paste' to change and add adjectives.

## Display ideas

Make a display of adjectives and ask the children to draw cartoons to illustrate their meanings by showing examples of people or objects with particular characteristics. Encourage the children to add to the display as they discover new adjectives through their reading.

## Other aspects of the English PoS covered

Speaking and listening – 3b.
Reading – 3.

## Reference to photocopiable sheet

Photocopiable page 110 provides a passage containing bland adjectives which the children have to replace with a more descriptive selection.

# PLURALS (1)

***To understand the concept of pluralization and to develop a greater knowledge of regular and irregular noun plurals.***

†† *Whole-class work followed by individual or paired work.*

⊕ *At least one hour.*

## Previous skills/knowledge needed

Children will need to understand the terms *singular* and *plural*.

## Key background information

Regular plurals are formed by adding an *s* to the singular form. Most children have worked this out orally and apply the rule in speech even before they start school. However, there are many exceptions to the rule and it is these which present problems and often cause amusement. This activity is intended to introduce the terms *singular* and *plural,* and to provide children with the opportunity to look at some common irregular plurals.

*Literacy Hour:* a series of Literacy Hours could be developed for Y3 T2 (S5), with the focus on texts and children being asked to identify plurals within them.

## Preparation

Make sufficient copies of photocopiable page 111 and photocopiable page 112 according to the abilities of the children in your class.

## Resources needed

Photocopiable pages 111 and 112, board or flip chart, writing materials.

## What to do

*Introduction*

Begin by using tangible items such as chairs, pencils, books and even children to ask the children to change given singular forms of words to plurals. They will find this simple, especially if you stick to regular plurals. Write the words *singular* and *plural* on the board and ask the children to give examples of singulars which you can write under the first heading. Ask them to tell you the plurals, and write them in a parallel column.

Ask the children to tell you what the rule is for turning singulars into plurals, and then ask them if there are any exceptions. You could start by asking what the plural of *child* is. Go on to look at sets of plurals which conform to rules. For example: *brushes, bushes, watches, churches; tomatoes, potatoes, echoes, heroes; babies, ladies, lilies, stories; monkeys, donkeys, keys; lives, wives, loaves, leaves.*

Encourage the children to try to work out what the rules are for the sets of plurals, and to look closely at the words to find out what distinguishes one type of word from another. For example, get them to look at the words which end with *h* (such as *bush* and *brush*) and ask them how the plural is formed, and then write a rule such as 'Words which end with *h* add *es* when they are made into plurals'.

To help the children to work out the plurals of words ending with *y*, you could tell them that the word *key* is the 'key' to remembering. They should all know that the plural of *key* is *keys*, not *kies*, and if they remember that, they should be able to work out that words which have a vowel before *y* add an *s* in the plural, but words with a consonant (such as *baby*) drop the *y* and add *ies*.

*Individual/group work*

Ask the children to match the singulars and plurals on photocopiable page 111. Some children may begin by working on the second sheet, provided on photocopiable page 112, while others may move on to it when they have finished the first one satisfactorily.

Before they begin the second sheet, go through a couple of examples of sentences which would need a change in the verb form if a noun was made plural. Encourage them to look at what they should do to some verbs when singulars become plurals. When they have done this, ask them to make up sentences with singular nouns and then rewrite them with plural nouns.

**Suggestion(s) for extension**

More able children could focus on photocopiable page 112 and discuss whether there are possible alternative answers. For example, *The girl is sitting on a sofa* could become *The girls are sitting on sofas* or *The girls are sitting on a sofa*.

Some words are the same in the plural and the singular. These include names of fish such as *salmon* and *trout*, and some other animals such as *deer* and *sheep*. (Note that the plural of *fish* can be *fish* or *fishes*.) The children could research nouns whose singular form may also be used as a plural and make a collection of them, together with other unusual plurals, using dictionaries and asking adults at home for words that fall into this category.

**Suggestion(s) for support**

Children who struggle with the concepts of singular and plural may benefit from additional oral work followed by shared writing of plurals with an adult. They could focus on photocopiable page 111 only, rather than going on to the more difficult activity on page 112.

**Assessment opportunities**

Look for evidence that children understand the concepts of singular and plural and are able to change nouns appropriately.

**Opportunities for IT**

Suggest that children use the spellchecker to see if their suggestions for plurals are correct.

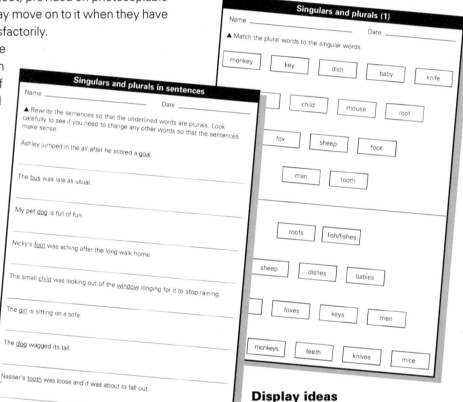

**Display ideas**

Make a display of irregular plurals and allow the children to add to it as they discover more. The display might incorporate illustrations which show 'one' and 'more than one' of each item.

**Other aspects of the English PoS covered**

Reading – 3.

Speaking and listening – 3a.

**Reference to photocopiable sheets**

Photocopiable pages 111 and 112 both relate to the use of plurals. Page 111 is a word activity on matching singular and plural nouns. Page 112 is a more demanding sentence-level activity involving the pluralization of verbs and pronouns with pluralized nouns.

# PLURALS (2)

*To understand the concept of pluralization and to develop a greater knowledge of regular and irregular noun plurals.*

†† *Whole-class work followed by individual or paired work.*

🕐 *At least one hour.*

## Previous skills/knowledge needed

Children should have successfully completed work on the previous activity, 'Plurals (1)' (page 65), before attempting this activity.

## Key background information

In this activity children look at the effects upon other words in a sentence when they are changing singular forms of words to plurals. It is a development of the previous activity and requires children to look at extended pieces of text to make plurals, ensuring that subjects and verbs agree.

*Literacy Hour:* this activity could be part of a series of Literacy Hours for Y3 T2 (S11) which focus on grammatical agreement.

## Preparation

Compile a list of words which have irregular plurals. Make copies of photocopiable page 113, an enlarged copy for the introductory work and one copy for each child or pair of children.

## Resources needed

Photocopiable page 113, paper, writing materials.

## What to do

### Introduction

Talk again about singulars and plurals and show the children some singulars which have irregular plurals, asking them to suggest what these might be. For example: *foot (feet)*, *penny* (which could become *pennies* or *pence* – it is *pennies* when we talk about separate coins as in 'You have to save your pennies' and *pence* when we talk about

quantities of money as in 'The sweets cost twenty pence'), *brother-in-law (brothers-in-law)*, *innings (innings* – the same in the plural as in the singular). Some children may have brought in lists of unusual plurals as part of the extension work from the previous activity. If so, use the opportunity to discuss some of the words.

Now show the children a piece of text which has several nouns underlined and ask them to look at it with you and change the singulars to plurals. When they have done this, ask them to look at the verbs to see if any need to be changed so that they agree with the subject nouns. They should also notice that some other words besides verbs may need to change if the text is to make sense. For example, in *The squirrel hid its acorns* we need to change *its* to *their* if we make *squirrel* plural.

The first paragraph of photocopiable page 113 may be useful for the above; but leave plenty of text for the children to work on during individual and group work.

### Individual/group work

Ask the children to work through the text on photocopiable page 113, orally in pairs, before going on to make corrections on the sheet. They should not be asked to copy the sheet out, as the main objective is to develop their understanding of plurals rather than to provide handwriting practice. Because changing the nouns to plurals affects pronouns and verbs, children may need guidance if they are to complete the task successfully. Stop them occasionally and discuss the changes which different pairs have made.

### Suggestion(s) for extension

Ask some children to look at other texts and experiment with changing singulars to plurals and vice versa. Encourage them to explore the effects that this has upon the whole text. For example, if the first noun is pluralized in the following sentence, it is necessary to make changes to other words: *The man wore a red coat and a black hat. The men wore red coats and black hats.*

## Suggestion(s) for support

Children who find working with the text difficult could be given short and simple sentences similar to those given on the photocopiable sheet, but written as individual sentences in a list, rather than in continuous prose.

## Assessment opportunities

Look for evidence that children are aware that changing singular nouns to plurals affects other words in the text.

## Opportunities for IT

Reproduce the text as a file, remembering to make back-up copies, and ask some children to make the changes by editing on screen.

## Display ideas

Make one set of cards with singular nouns and another with matching plurals. Children could be asked to match the cards and to find other examples of pairs which have similar forms.

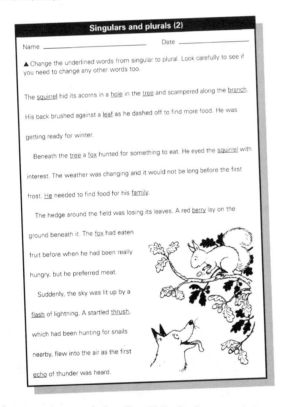

## Other aspects of the English PoS covered

Reading – 3.
Speaking and listening – 3a.

## Reference to photocopiable sheet

Photocopiable page 113 shows a passage of text incorporating several singular nouns. The children amend the text by changing the nouns which are underlined into plurals and then pluralizing other words so that they agree with the nouns. Only one noun is underlined in each sentence, but sometimes the children may need to change other nouns into plurals.

# SUBORDINATE CLAUSES AND PHRASES

*To understand the value of subordinate clauses and phrases and to be able to make use of them in writing.*

†† *Whole-class work followed by individual or paired work.*

🕐 *At least one hour.*

## Previous skills/knowledge needed

Children will need to understand the terms *subordinate*, *clause* and *phrase*.

## Key background information

Subordinate clauses and phrases can enhance writing by giving additional information without the need to provide it in a separate sentence.
For example: *Daniel was a good cricketer. His father had played for Yorkshire.*
could be written as: *Daniel, whose father had played for Yorkshire, was a good cricketer.*

The use of the subordinate clause here makes writing less stilted and allows it to flow. When discussing the use of subordinate clauses and phrases it is important to explain:

▲ *subordinate* means less important or lower down the order

▲ a *clause* contains a verb

▲ a *phrase* does not contain a verb

▲ the word which connects the clause to the main sentence is a *relative pronoun* (for example *who*, *which*, *whose*) or a subordinating conjunction (for example *but*, *while*).

*Literacy Hour:* this lesson could form part of a series of Literacy Hours for Y6 for Terms 1 (S5), 2 (S3) or 3 (S3), which focus on complex sentences.

## Preparation

Find examples of subordinate clauses and phrases in texts with which the children are familiar and copy some of these in large writing. Make one copy per child of photocopiable page 114, and some copies of photocopiable page 115 (see 'Suggestions(s) for support').

## Resources needed

Copies of examples of the use of subordinates taken from children's books, photocopiable pages 114 and 115, board or flip chart, writing materials.

## What to do

*Introduction*

Show the children examples of sentences which include subordinates and ask them to look at them closely and read them aloud. Encourage them to look at the punctuation and ask them what the main messages in the sentences are. Ask them which parts of the sentences could be left out without affecting the meaning of the main part of the sentence. Explain to them that these are *subordinates*. You could explain the meaning of *subordinate* by discussing ranks in an organization.

Show the children some more sentences and ask them to identify the subordinates, and then show them some sentences which do not have subordinates and ask them to think of possible subordinate phrases or clauses which could add meaning if included within the sentences. Emphasize the need to use commas to separate the main clause from the subordinate. For example: *Doncaster, which is the home of the St Leger horse race, was once famous for coal-mining.*

### Individual/group work

Provide the children with copies of photocopiable page 114 and ask them to try to combine the sentences in each example to produce one sentence. Emphasize that there may be different ways in which this could be done.
For example: *Rachel loved climbing trees. She was always coming home with dirty clothes.*
could become: *Rachel, who loved climbing trees, was always coming home with dirty clothes.*
or: *Rachel, who was always coming home with dirty clothes, loved climbing trees.*

Stop the class occasionally to draw attention to the different ways in which children have approached the task, and write some of their sentences on the board and discuss them.

### Suggestion(s) for extension

Some groups could write their own sentences which include subordinates, or could be asked to write passages of prose which include them.

### Suggestion(s) for support

Children who are struggling with the concept of subordinates could use photocopiable page 115, which has a set of main sentences and a set of subordinates which can be matched to them. Again, emphasize that there may be different combinations which would make sense.

### Assessment opportunities

Note the children's abilities to make use of subordinates accurately and imaginatively. Ask individuals to tell you about the subordinates they have used and look for clear signs that they understand the concept.

### Opportunities for IT

Provide passages of text which children can manipulate on the word processor, combining shorter sentences to make longer ones or breaking up complex sentences into shorter constituent sentences.

### Display ideas

Display examples of the children's sentences, together with highlighted examples on copies of pages from well-known children's books.

### Other aspects of the English PoS covered

Reading – 3.
Speaking and listening – 3a.

### Reference to photocopiable sheets

Photocopiable page 114 shows eight pairs of sentences: the children have to combine each pair into a single sentence with a subordinate clause or phrase. Photocopiable page 115 shows an easier task which can be used for support: the children have to match five subordinate clauses to the appropriate main sentences.

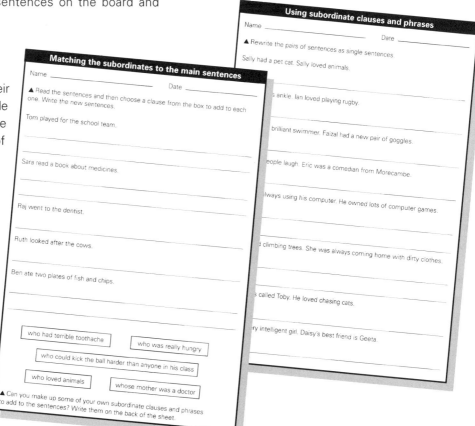

# PAST TENSE

***To understand the concept of the past tense and the present tense.***

†† *Whole-class work followed by individual or paired work.*

🕐 *At least one hour.*

## Previous skills/knowledge needed

Children should be familiar with the terms *past* and *present*.

## Key background information

In this activity the children explore ways of changing text written in the past tense into the present tense. A common problem in children's writing is the inappropriate mixing of tenses. The text on photocopiable page 116 is written in the present continuous tense (it is an ongoing pattern rather than something which is happening at a particular time) and can easily be changed into the past tense.

*Literacy Hour:* this activity could be part of a series of Literacy Hours for Y4 in T3 (S3) which focus on how the grammar of sentences alters when the sentence type is changed.

## Preparation

Make an enlarged copy of photocopiable page 116 and sufficient copies for children to have one between two. Find some examples of text from books which are well-known to the children and be prepared to read short extracts that are written in the past tense.

## Resources needed

Examples of writing in the past tense, photocopiable page 116, board or flip chart, paper, writing materials.

## What to do

*Introduction*

Read the passage 'A day in Oxford' to the children and ask them if they have any comments on the content. Then ask them to make up questions for each other about the passage. The questions may well be phrased in the past tense, as this is the tense most commonly used in narrative. The answers may also be given in the past tense. If this happens, ask the children whether the visit has already happened or is to happen in the future.

Read some extracts from stories and ask the children about the differences in tense between these and the text 'A day in Oxford'.

Explain that you would like the children to help you to change the text in 'A day in Oxford' into the past tense. Look at the opening paragraph with them and read it aloud, before asking the children to re-read it in their heads and to think about what would need to be changed. Begin by changing the opening sentence to *Last Saturday we went to Oxford* and then ask the children to look at the rest of the paragraph. Invite their suggestions and write these on the board. You may wish to show the children an example of how the text could be changed, but you should emphasize that there is no one correct way in which to do this. The following example may be helpful: *Last Saturday we went to Oxford. We travelled by car and parked at the Park and Ride car park. We took the bus into the centre of the city.*

*Individual/group work*

Ask the children to work in pairs on copies of the photocopiable sheet to continue to change the passage into the past tense. Encourage them to discuss their work, and make a point of stopping the class occasionally to discuss the ways in which they have tackled the task.

### Suggestion(s) for extension

Some children could go on to write additional paragraphs for the text, using the past tense.

### Suggestion(s) for support

You may need to provide examples of past tense versions of some of the present tense verbs in the passage, to support some children. Oral work with an adult will be particularly helpful for those who find the task difficult.

## Assessment opportunities

Look for evidence that children understand the difference between the past and present tenses and are able to write in the appropriate tense consistently.

## Opportunities for IT

Present the text in a file, remembering to make back-up copies, and ask children to use 'cut', 'paste' and 'edit' to change its tense.

## Display ideas

Find examples of text which is written in the present tense. Some early reading scheme books are written in the present tense and may be useful here. Display these, together with a copy of the photocopiable sheet and some examples of the children's revised versions. The display could be a useful source of group activities for the Literacy Hour, if children are asked to change some of the present tense texts into the past.

## Other aspects of the English PoS covered

Speaking and listening – 3a.
Reading – 3.

## Reference to photocopiable sheet

Photocopiable page 116 shows a passage written in the present tense. The children can explore ways of rewriting it in the past tense.

# VERB EXCHANGE

***To identify verbs and replace them with alternative verbs.***

†† *Whole-class work followed by paired work.*
🕐 *At least one hour.*

## Previous skills/knowledge needed

The children will need to understand the concept of a verb, and it will be helpful if they have had experience of identifying verbs within sentences.

## Key background information

This activity focuses children's attentions on verbs and their usage. It allows them to pick out the verbs in a text and then attempt to replace them with alternatives. Despite being the most common verb and the starting point for sentences when we learn a foreign language, the verb 'to be' is often the one which children find hardest to identify. The fact that it is irregular may have an effect, or it may be that children use the verb so often from an early age that they never really think about it as a part of speech. When trying to find a replacement for a part of the verb 'to be' children may have to change the tense rather than the verb, since to do otherwise would often render a sentence nonsensical.

For example: for *Mushtaq is a good tennis player.*
there are few alternatives to: *Mushtaq was a good tennis player.*

It would be difficult to replace the verb 'to be' in such a sentence, but changing from *is* to *was* during a whole-class introduction would provide an opportunity to discuss tenses with the children.

*Literacy Hour:* this work could be used in Y3, especially in Term 1 (S3) when children learn to use the term *verb* appropriately and to understand and use verb tenses with increasing accuracy.

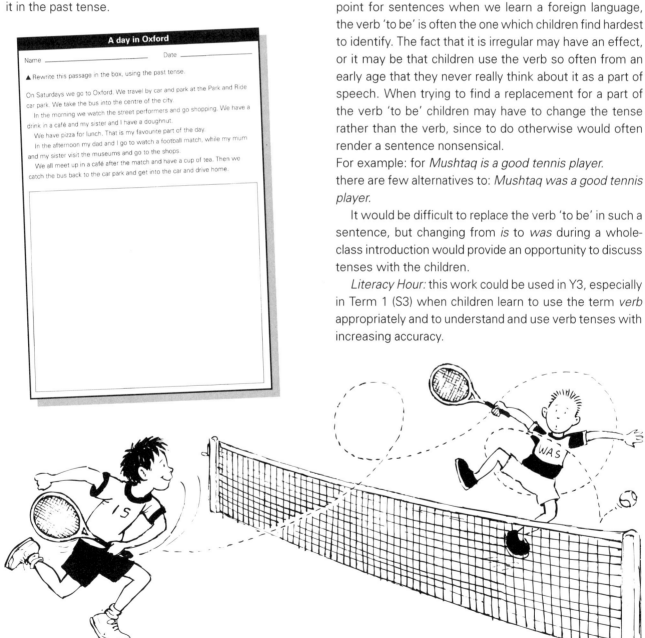

### A day in Oxford

Name _____ Date _____

▲ Rewrite this passage in the box, using the past tense.

On Saturdays we go to Oxford. We travel by car and park at the Park and Ride car park. We take the bus into the centre of the city.

In the morning we watch the street performers and go shopping. We have a drink in a café and my sister and I have a doughnut.

We have pizza for lunch. That is my favourite part of the day.

In the afternoon my dad and I go to watch a football match, while my mum and my sister visit the museums and go to the shops.

We all meet up in a café after the match and have a cup of tea. Then we catch the bus back to the car park and get into the car and drive home.

## Preparation

Make copies of photocopiable page 117, one per pair. Write some simple sentences on the board. These should include a single verb initially. Choose sentences that include verbs with which the children are familiar and which could easily be replaced by several alternatives. For example: *Mr Singh kicked the ball*. The verb *kicked* could be replaced by *threw, tossed, rolled, headed, caught* and so on. Further examples of sentences could be suggested by the children.

## Resources needed

Photocopiable page 117, board or flip chart, writing materials.

## What to do

### Introduction

Show the children the sentences on the board and ask if anyone can tell you what is being done in each one. You could ask children to perform certain actions and then write sentences on the board to describe what they are doing, inviting the class to identify the verbs. For example: *Jon stood up. Chloe scratched her head. Rupa whispered something to Luke.*

Discuss the verbs with the children and ask them to try to replace them with alternatives. The children involved could then act out the revised actions. For example: *Jon jumped up. Chloe nodded her head. Rupa shouted something to Luke.*

You may feel that it is worthwhile discussing the tenses of the verbs with the children and asking them to provide replacements which are in the same tenses as the original verbs, as in the examples above. This would, however, be difficult for the verb 'to be' in many cases, so where this is part of a sentence you might ask children to change the tense. You could use a sentence similar to the last one on photocopiable page 117 as an example.

### Individual/group work

Provide copies of photocopiable page 117 for pairs of children and ask them to replace the verbs, writing the new verbs under the originals and ensuring that their sentences make sense.

Stop the class occasionally to discuss the verbs they have used. Pay special attention to any inventive and new vocabulary and make a point of showing the children how to spell such words.

## Suggestion(s) for extension

Ask the children to work in pairs to write sentences for each other to change. You could also ask children to take a familiar piece of text and change some or all of the verbs, and then read it to the class.

## Suggestion(s) for support

Provide some alternative verbs for those children who find the activity difficult, and ask them to choose the verb replacements from your selection. Verbs could include: *ran, jumped, smiled, understood, headed, roared, kicked, dropped, laughed, spilled, fell, howled, was, cleaning.*

## Assessment opportunities

Look for clear signs that children understand what a verb is and can recognize verbs in their reading.

## Opportunities for IT

The text used by the more able children could be provided as a file, so that children could use the 'cut' and 'paste' facilities to replace the verbs.

## Display ideas

Display a selection of commonly used verbs and then ask the children to write alternatives on pieces of card, which can be displayed next to the original verbs.

## Other aspects of the English PoS covered

Speaking and listening – 3a.
Reading – 3.

### Replace the verbs

Name _____

Date _____

▲ Identify the verbs in the sentences and then replace them with different verbs.

Peter walked down the road.

Jane climbed over a fence.

Sasha laughed when she heard the joke.

Ali kicked the ball into the goal as the crowd cheered.

Lewis threw the ball to Megan and she caught it.

Kate giggled as she dropped her dinner on to the floor.

The rain poured from the dark clouds and the wind blew strongly.

Matthew is one of the cleverest children in the class at using a computer but he is hopeless at tidying his room.

## Reference to photocopiable sheet

Photocopiable page 117 shows eight sentences of varying complexity. The children have to identify the verbs in each sentence and find appropriate alternatives for them.

# PROOFREADING

*To make use of prompts to revise and edit a piece of prose.*

†† *Whole-class work followed by individual or paired work.*

🕐 *At least one hour.*

## Previous skills/knowledge needed

Children will need to be aware of the importance of reading through their work to check for errors. It would be helpful if they have already experienced proofreading that focuses on particular aspects of writing such as full stops and capital letters.

## Key background information

Children are often asked to check their work before showing it to the teacher. This is sometimes ineffective, as the children may not be sure about what exactly they need to check. This activity allows them to focus attention on a few key elements; if they are given a list of things that they should look out for, they will find proofreading much easier.

*Literacy Hour:* this activity could be developed into part of a series of Literacy Hours for Y3 T2 (S6, S7, S8) focusing on various aspects of word- and sentence-level work. It could then be linked to extended writing if checklists are provided for children's proofreading of such work.

## Preparation

Write a short piece of text which includes some quite obvious inaccuracies, and display it for the children to read. Compile a list of the things that you would like the children to look out for in the text. Make one copy per child of photocopiable page 118, and also an enlarged copy.

## Resources needed

A short passage which includes obvious mistakes, accompanying list (explaining how to search for errors when proofreading), photocopiable page 118, paper, writing materials.

## What to do

### Introduction

Ask the children to look at the passage which you have written, and work with them to correct it, referring to your list of proofreading points. Read through the text together, discussing the different things that they should be trying to find (it may be easier to deal with one type of error at a time).

Now show the children part of the text on the enlarged copy of photocopiable page 118 and ask them for their comments. Look at the checklist at the foot of the page with them and ensure that they understand what is being asked of them.

### Individual/group work

Provide copies of photocopiable page 118, one for each child or pair, and ask them to correct the mistakes, using the checklist to guide them. They should not rewrite the text, but should use a distinctively coloured pen or pencil to highlight the errors and correct them.

Stop the class occasionally to discuss the errors which have been identified.

## Suggestion(s) for extension

Ask the children to make copies of their own work, which they have carried out at the computer in a previous lesson, and to insert mistakes for others to correct. It is important that they retain the correct version and that they understand the errors they have made.

## Suggestion(s) for support

Some children may need a shorter and simpler passage on which to work, or they could work on a set of individual sentences. Limit the number of errors in the sentences and focus on a small number of features of grammar or spelling.

## Assessment opportunities

Note children's abilities not only to spot mistakes and correct them, but also to explain the errors and apply their knowledge to other incorrect texts. This may be done through discussions with the children both individually and as a group during a plenary session.

## Opportunities for IT
See 'Suggestion(s) for extension'.

## Display ideas
Make a checklist for display each time children write at length. There may be some things which you will always wish to include, such as capital letters at the beginning of sentences and full stops at the end. Other features, such as using speech marks or consistency with tenses, may be used when they are the focus of attention for a particular piece of writing.

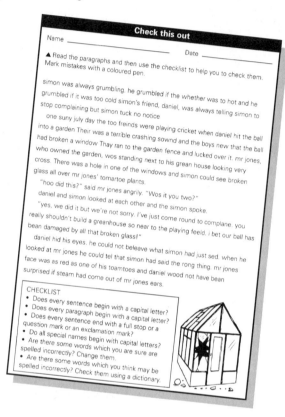

## Other aspects of the English PoS covered
Reading – 3.
Speaking and listening – 3a.

## Reference to photocopiable sheet
Photocopiable page 118 shows a passage which contains many spelling and punctuation errors, and a checklist of points to which the children can refer when proofreading the text.

# CONFUSING SENTENCES
***To understand how clauses and phrases can be manipulated to achieve different effects.***
†† *Whole-class work followed by paired work.*
🕐 *At least one hour.*

## Previous skills/knowledge needed
Children will need to understand what clauses and phrases are.

## Key background information
In this activity children are asked to look at sentences which, though apparently grammatically correct, lead to confusion because of their structure. The work provides an opportunity for them to develop an understanding of the ways in which clauses can be manipulated to achieve different effects.
*Literacy Hour:* Y5 T2 (S 7), Y6 T1 (S1, S3, S5) and Y6 T3 (S4) all have objectives which could be met through this activity.

## Preparation
Make an enlarged copy of photocopiable page 119 and either make multiple copies or ensure that the enlargement may be displayed throughout the lesson, so that everyone can see it and work from it.

## Resources needed
Photocopiable page 119, paper, board or flip chart, writing materials.

## What to do
*Introduction*
Make up some examples of confusing sentences and write them on the board. Ask the children to read them and to tell you what the writer is trying to convey, and what the reader has actually been told. Can the children suggest other ways of phrasing the sentences, by moving clauses, changing the wording, or both? For example:
*Sally travelled from Hull to Doncaster in her best suit.*
*Wearing her best suit, Sally travelled from Hull to Doncaster.*
*Sally wore her best suit when she travelled from Hull to Doncaster.*
Work on the sentences on the enlarged version of photocopiable page 119 until you feel that the children can see where they might be confusing and are confident enough to attempt to change them.

## Individual/group work

Give each pair of children a copy of photocopiable page 119 or let them work from the enlarged version. Explain that you would like the children to look at the sentences, decide what the author really meant to say, and then rewrite them on a separate sheet of paper. They could change the order of the words and/or change the words themselves. Encourage them to discuss possible changes, and to make several attempts to change the sentences if they feel this is necessary. The emphasis should be on their ability to manipulate word order rather than attractive presentation at this stage.

Stop the class occasionally to allow children to compare notes on their different approaches to changing the sentences, and so that you can offer help and guidance.

## Suggestion(s) for extension

Children who complete the work successfully could try making up their own confusing sentences for others to reorganize. As part of an art lesson, they could go on to draw cartoons which depict the ridiculous scenarios suggested by some of the confusing sentences.

## Suggestion(s) for support

Children who experience problems could be given simpler sentences and might work with an adult or with the teacher. For example: *The girl hit the boy with a ball.*

## Assessment opportunities

Look for evidence that children understand that word order and punctuation affect meaning and that they can manipulate words, phrases and clauses to achieve different effects.

## Opportunities for IT

The sentences on photocopiable page 119 could be typed into files (make back-up copies) and children could manipulate them using 'cut' and 'paste'.

## Display ideas

Display some confusing sentences written by the children, together with others that you and they discover (joke books are a good source). Add some cartoon depictions of the confused meanings. Use the display as a resource for children to work from, as part of a series of Literacy Hours.

## Other aspects of the English PoS covered

Reading – 3.
Speaking and listening – 3a.

## Reference to photocopiable sheet

Photocopiable page 119 shows a selection of ambiguous sentences. The children have to suggest ways of restructuring or rewording them to remove the ambiguity.

**Confusing sentences**

▲ Can you tell what the sentences tell us in their present form? Can you rewrite them so that they make more sense?

"I'm looking for a really good girl's coat," said Caitlin.

Ryan pushed Bill in his kitchen.

Mr Aldridge spent two hours shooting at his farm.

Kyle was going to pass the ball but decided to shoot himself instead.

Saffi hid from her sister in her favourite jumper.

Mrs Murphy sailed to the Isle of Man in a blue dress.

Sam taught his dog to do tricks better than his father.

Hayley had a third child called Edward.

The boxer was a tall man with a broken nose called Henry.

Helping himself to a cake, Kieran walked to the door and popped it in his mouth.

Alistair opened the door in his pyjamas.

## SIMPLE ENGLISH

*To understand the importance of choosing appropriate vocabulary for a younger audience and to make use of reference sources.*

†† *Whole-class work followed by paired work.*

🕐 *At least one hour.*

### Previous skills/knowledge needed

Children should have discussed examples of complex sentences and should have experience of editing and revising them.

### Key background information

Sometimes sentences are constructed in a convoluted way in order to achieve a literary effect. Examples might include: *She was no stranger to a jam doughnut. He was not unfamiliar with the experience of having to remain behind after school.*

However, often words are used in an unnecessary and tautologous way and children need to develop the skill of being concise. In this activity examples of repetition and 'waffle' are presented for children to modify.

*Literacy Hour:* this lesson could be developed into Literacy Hours for Y5 in T2 and could be part of a series which focuses on constructing sentences in different ways (S8).

### Preparation

Make an enlarged copy of photocopiable page 120 and either make multiple copies or ensure that the enlargement is displayed throughout the lesson, so that everyone can see it and work from it.

### Resources needed

Photocopiable page 120, paper, board or flip chart, writing materials.

### What to do

*Introduction*

Show the children an enlarged copy of photocopiable page 120. Ask them to read the sentences with you. Now ask them to tell you what information is given in each sentence, and invite them to suggest a simpler way of putting it. The sentences are reproduced below, together with suggestions for revised versions. It is important that the children realize that there are many different ways of expressing the same idea, and that there is no one correct way to rewrite each sentence.

I myself personally think that it is not unlikely that rain will fall tomorrow.
*I think it is likely to rain tomorrow.*
At this present moment in time we have an ongoing period of sunshine.
*It is sunny.*
Both of the two twins wore red jumpers.
*The twins wore red jumpers.*
Each and every person in the class had to stay in at playtime.
*Everyone had to stay in at playtime.*
Sasha has got a new bicycle and Daniel has got one too.
*Sasha and Daniel have new bicycles.*
"I have not got any money," said Tim.
*"I have no money," said Tim.*
In spite of the fact that it was raining, Ruth had not got her hat on.
*Despite the rain, Ruth had no hat.*
On the day before this one the sun shone in the sky.
*It was sunny yesterday.*
In the month which comes between March and May the weather began to change for the better.
*The weather improved in April.*

Emphasize to the children that, while it is often appropriate to write concisely, there are times when writing is more interesting if it is a little more convoluted. Provide some examples of this to explain how humour can be injected in this way.

*Individual/group work*

Provide copies of photocopiable page 120, one for each child or pair, or display the enlarged version. Ask the children to rewrite the sentences in a more concise way, writing their answers on the sheet.

Stop the class occasionally to discuss the ways in which the children have attempted the task. Write some examples of their revised sentences on the board and ask the children if they retain their original meanings.

## Suggestion(s) for extension

Children could look at sentences in books in the classroom and decide if any would be improved by being shortened.

## Suggestion(s) for support

This activity could be done as a guided writing session with children who need support work.

## Assessment opportunities

Look for evidence that children are able to construct sentences in different ways while retaining their meaning.

## Opportunities for IT

The sentences on photocopiable 120 could be keyed in at the computer (make back-up copies) and children could edit them, writing improved shorter versions.

## Display ideas

Display an enlarged copy of each of the original sentences together with the children's amended versions.

## Other aspects of the English PoS covered

Reading – 3.
Speaking and listening – 3a.

## Reference to photocopiable sheet

Photocopiable page 120 shows nine sentences which are written in a verbose and convoluted manner. The children have to rewrite each sentence in a simpler and clearer form.

# PRESENTATION

*To use a style of handwriting appropriate for presenting an attractive piece of work.*

✠ *Whole-class work followed by individual work.*
🕐 *At least one hour.*

## Previous skills/knowledge needed

Children should have seen examples of different styles of handwriting and of well-presented written work. These might be collected from previous classes or from colleagues' classes.

## Key background information

Children should come to realize that different types of handwriting are appropriate at different times depending upon the nature of the writing that they are doing and its intended audience. For example, they might use abbreviations and write quickly with less attention to neatness when making notes or drafting than when writing a poem which will be displayed on the classroom wall.

*Literacy Hour:* this activity would be particularly appropriate for Y4 in either T1 (W16) or T2 (W16).

## Preparation

Make a collection of different types of handwriting including rough notes, early stages of drafting, and final copies of formal letters and poems written for display. Examples of children's work will be particularly useful. Collect some short published poems (less than a page long).

## Resources needed

Examples of different writing (see 'Preparation'), a selection of short poems, paper, writing materials.

## What to do

*Introduction*

Show the children examples of different handwriting used in different circumstances and discuss with them when it would be appropriate to use each. While you should make it clear that best handwriting is used for work which is to be presented to others or for display, it is important not to be seen to be encouraging messy writing at other times.

Show some examples of poems which have been written attractively, and discuss the layout and the handwriting. Talk about the way in which each new line of a poem usually begins with a capital letter, even when it is not a new sentence. You may wish to show some examples of poetry which is set out in unconventional ways too, to show how poets sometimes make up their own rules. Michael Rosen and Brian Patten, for example, often write in unconventional ways.

### Individual/group work

Provide the children with a selection of poems which are no longer than a single page each, and ask them to copy them out carefully by hand. Encourage them to plan their writing to ensure that the poem will fit onto the page. The finished poems can be placed in a class anthology (see 'Display ideas').

### Suggestion(s) for extension

Some children could go on to choose further poems to write out and could learn them by heart for presentation to the class, or as part of an assembly.

### Suggestion(s) for support

Many children experience problems with fine motor skills and some are dyslexic or dyspraxic, or have other conditions which make it difficult for them to write neatly. Make sure that such children have shorter poems to write and consider providing them with faint pencil versions to write over. They may also need line guides to help them to keep their writing straight. Be prepared to accept work which is less well-presented from such children but praise them for their efforts.

### Assessment opportunities

Look for evidence of consistency in size and proportion of letters and for correct letter formation, as well as for accurate use of basic joins.

### Opportunities for IT

Although the writing in this lesson should be done by hand, you may feel it appropriate to allow some children who have particular problems with presentation to reproduce their poems using a word processor, once they have attempted to write them by hand. They might also scan examples of good handwriting onto pages alongside printed versions.

### Display ideas

Mount the poems onto separate sheets of different coloured paper and compile a class anthology. In an art lesson the children could add illustrations to the text and create a front and back cover.

### Other aspects of the English PoS covered

Reading – 1d.

# APOSTROPHES

*To understand the correct usage of apostrophes for elision and possession.*

†† *Whole-class work followed by individual work.*

🕐 *At least one hour.*

### Previous skills/knowledge needed

Children will probably have begun to use apostrophes in their work, but may be unsure about their correct usage.

### Key background information

Apostrophes are often misused and are a source of confusion for both children and adults. They show that something is missing and mark the place where letters are omitted. For example, in *don't* and *shouldn't* the apostrophes show the place where the *o* would be placed in *do not* and *should not* respectively. Teaching children about apostrophes presents an opportunity to discuss abbreviated forms and when it is appropriate to use them.

We tend to use shortened versions of *do not, should not* and so on in speech, and so children could be taught to limit their use to text within speech marks. A common mistake is to misplace apostrophes in abbreviated forms, so time spent talking about missing letters will be valuable.

Apostrophes used to denote possession also denote missing letters, but these have disappeared as the language has changed over time. In *David's hair*, for example, the longer version would once have been *David his hair* or *Davides hair*, while in *the boys' clothes* we once had *the boys their clothes*. Once children understand that the apostrophe shows where letters were once placed, it should be easier for them to place them correctly.

*Literacy Hour:* this lesson could form part of a series of Literacy Hours for Y4 T2 (S2) or Y5 T3 (S5). In each case, apostrophes should be studied in the context of extended texts.

### Preparation

In advance of the lesson, ask the children to look at shops and signs and make a note of words they find with apostrophes. Make one copy of photocopiable pages 121 and 122 for each child.

### Resources needed
Examples of the correct and incorrect use of apostrophes, photocopiable pages 121 and 122, paper, writing materials.

### What to do
*Introduction*
Begin by showing the children examples of words which include apostrophes. Show them correct versions first and ask them to explain why they think the apostrophes have been included. Help them to work out rules for using apostrophes to show omission.

Go on to discuss the use of apostrophes for possession, and illustrate the teaching points by referring to things which the children own. For example: *Nicholas's jumper, Kylie's coat, Ashi's CD player, the boys' cloakroom, the girls' toilets.*

Try turning sentences around to make it clear how many people own things and where apostrophes should be placed. For example: *the jumper belonging to Nicholas, the coat belonging to Kylie, the CD player belonging to Ashi, the cloakroom for the boys, the toilets for the girls.*

*Individual/group work*
Distribute copies of photocopiable page 121 and ask the children to look at it and to read it through carefully before deciding which apostrophes are correctly placed and which need to be changed or eliminated. Explain that they should write correct versions above the mistakes and tick correct usages.

Where children encounter problems, stop the class to discuss them and to make teaching points. When they have finished, ask the children to check their corrections against the correct version (photocopiable page 122) and to try to work out why they were right or wrong in each case.

### Suggestion(s) for extension
Some children could work in pairs to look through books to find examples of apostrophes and to decide whether the apostrophe shows possession, or is used to shorten a word or to combine words.

### Suggestion(s) for support
Children who struggle with the use of apostrophes could be given work which focuses on apostrophes for elision.

They could be given a list of examples such as *didn't, wouldn't, can't* and *don't* and asked to write the full versions, and then to shorten or combine other words by using apostrophes.

### Assessment opportunities
Look for evidence that children understand the use of apostrophes for elision and for showing possession.

### Display ideas
Make a display of correct and incorrect usage of apostrophes and label each example to show whether it is correct or incorrect and to explain why.

### Other aspects of the English PoS covered
Reading – 3.
Speaking and listening – 3a.

### Reference to photocopiable sheets
Photocopiable page 121 shows a passage of text with several apostrophes missing or misplaced. The children mark corrections on the sheet, then compare it to the corrected version on photocopiable page 122.

# CHANGING SENTENCES

***To understand how the grammar of a sentence alters when the sentence type is changed.***

†† *Whole-class work followed by paired work.*

🕐 *At least one hour.*

## Previous skills/knowledge needed

Children should be aware of question sentences and should understand the term *negative*.

## Key background information

This activity focuses on the ways in which word order, tenses and punctuation change when sentences are adapted to become questions or negatives. A potentially dull exercise can become imaginative and enjoyable if the activity is developed beyond children simply rewriting sentences. They could go on to make up examples of their own or to change passages of prose (see 'Suggestion(s) for extension').

*Literacy Hour:* this activity could be part of a series of Literacy Hours for Y4 T3 which focus on word order (S3). It could be further developed to include changing tenses.

## Preparation

Find or make a set of cards with common words written on them. A *Breakthrough to Literacy* set by David Mackay *et al* (Longman) could be used. Make copies of photocopiable page 123, one for each pair.

## Resources needed

Photocopiable page 123, a set of word cards (see 'Preparation'), paper, board or flip chart, writing materials.

## What to do

*Introduction*

Begin by displaying a sentence in which each word is written on a separate piece of card. Try the following:

*Bethany is good at reading.*

Ask the children to turn the statement into a question and to move the words around to show how word order is affected. Encourage them to look at the way in which the punctuation changes and ask them to tell you if any of the words now needs a capital letter. Try this with other sentences and ask the children to make some up and write them on the board for others to change.

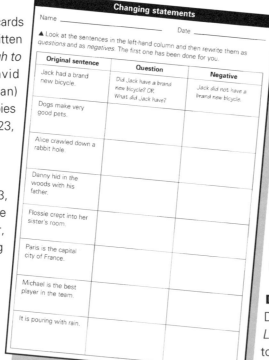

Now go back to the original sentence and ask the children to turn it into a negative statement. Have the word *not* ready for them to use, but accept other negatives such as *isn't*. This should provide an opportunity to reinforce the idea of abbreviated negatives being used in speech rather than in written prose.

*Individual/group work*

Provide each pair of children with a copy of photocopiable page 123 and ask them to turn each sentence into a question and then into a negative. They could then make up sentences for each other to change. Bring the class together at the end of the lesson to discuss some examples, and use the opportunity to talk again about the ways in which the grammar of a sentence changes when its sentence type changes.

## Suggestion(s) for extension

Provide children who manage the activity easily with a passage of prose and ask them to change its meaning from positive to negative.

## Suggestion(s) for support

Provide sets of word cards (*Breakthrough to Literacy* could be used or you could make your own) and make up sentences with the children's help. Ask them to move or add words to change the meanings. Only when they feel confident about this should they move on to written work.

## Assessment opportunities

Look for evidence that children understand how the grammar of a sentence changes when the sentence type is changed.

## Opportunities for IT

Children could work on the word processor to 'cut' and 'paste' words to change the meanings of sentences.

## Display ideas

Display a set of words or a *Breakthrough to Literacy* folder and sentence stand for children to use to practise changing word order and word choice in sentences.

## Other aspects of the English PoS covered

Reading – 3.

Speaking and listening – 3a.

## Reference to photocopiable sheet

Photocopiable page 123 shows several statements (including a worked example) which the children have to convert into questions and into opposing statements.

# ARRANGING SENTENCES

*To understand the importance of sentence order in establishing the meaning of a text.*

✝✝ *Whole-class work followed by individual or paired work.*

🕐 *At least one hour.*

## Previous skills/knowledge needed

Children should understand that text can be arranged in paragraphs to indicate changes in time, subject, place, speaker and so on.

## Key background information

This activity is designed to encourage children to look carefully at a piece of text and consider a logical order in which to arrange the sentences within it. They then sort the newly arranged text into paragraphs, with each paragraph representing a change of time.

If you have children from non-Christian faiths in your class, you may like to prepare a similar activity for their festivals.

## Preparation

Make enlarged copies of photocopiable page 124 and photocopiable page 125, as well as multiple copies of photocopiable page 124.

In advance of the lesson, discuss the children's family traditions at Christmas. You could let this lead into asking them to produce a piece of descriptive chronological writing before the activity.

*Literacy Hour:* Literacy Hours for Y4 in Term 2 could be developed from this lesson with a focus on word order (S3) and planning for writing (T12, T24).

## Resources needed

Photocopiable pages 124 and 125, paper, scissors, writing materials.

## What to do

*Introduction*

Talk with the children about some of the words which can be used to indicate a change of time. These include: *finally, next, after* and *eventually*.

Show them an example of a text (a story or an instructional text such as a recipe, for example) which includes such words and look at the ways in which the author has used these types of words as well as changes of paragraph to indicate changes in time.

Look with the children at the photocopiable sheet of the muddled text about Christmas Day traditions (photocopiable page 124) and read it with them. Ask them what they think is wrong with it and encourage them to suggest some changes to the order. Avoid rearranging the whole text – leave the children to do this in groups or pairs later.

*Individual/group work*

Provide the children with copies of the text on photocopiable page 124 and ask them to cut out the sentences, then sort them into what they consider to be a logical order. Ask them to put the sentences into groups which could be paragraphs.

They should not copy the text out, but could write headings for each paragraph or write an explanation for why they have arranged the sentences as they have.

Finally, show the children the 'correct' version of 'Family traditions at Christmas (2)' (page 125) and discuss the order of the paragraphs, asking the children to compare this version with their own ordering.

## Suggestion(s) for extension

Invite children who complete their work successfully to make notes about a typical Christmas Day in their house. They can then use their notes to write a story that is similar in format to the one provided on photocopiable page 125.

## Suggestion(s) for support

Some children could attempt this activity working with an adult or a more able partner. You may need to provide an alternative example of simpler text for some children, which is based upon the photocopiable sheet, but amended appropriately.

## Assessment opportunities

Look for evidence that children are able to look at the text critically and determine the most logical way in which to order it and divide it into paragraphs.

## Opportunities for IT

This activity is ideally suited to editing on a word processor. You could key in the text, making back-up copies of the file, and then ask children to use the 'cut' and 'paste' facilities to manipulate the text into a logical order.

## Display ideas

The rearranged text could be displayed alongside the muddled text, as part of a display on what children did at Christmas.

## Other aspects of the English PoS covered

Reading – 3.
Speaking and listening – 3a.

## Reference to photocopiable sheets

Photocopiable page 124 shows a passage of text in which the sentences have been placed in an illogical order. The children cut out and rearrange the sentences into a better order, then divide the text into paragraphs. Photocopiable page 125 provides a possible solution.

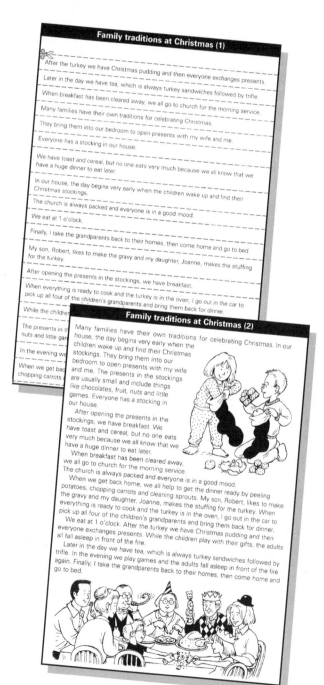

# ORGANIZING NOTES

***To use notes to draft writing.***

†† *Whole-class work followed by individual or paired work.*

🕐 *At least one hour.*

## Previous skills/knowledge needed

Children should have previous experience of making notes in preparation for writing.

## Key background information

This activity could be the prelude to others in which the children make notes and then use them as a starting point for extended writing. It provides a model for note-making and organizing writing, and it may best be done after the children have discussed a topic and notes have been made on the board. This could be carried out in a lesson immediately before the present one, or it could be done the day before in order to give you the opportunity to copy and reproduce the notes for the children.

*Literacy Hour:* this activity could form part of a series of Literacy Hours for Y5 T1 which focus on making notes and using them as a basis for extended writing (T26).

## Preparation

Ask the children to help you to make some notes on a topic which they are currently studying. Write their ideas on the board, as they are given. For example, if the topic is 'The countryside', write words and phrases such as:

| | |
|---|---|
| not very crowded | lots of farms |
| narrow lanes | small villages |
| farmyard smells | farm animals |
| footpaths | quiet |
| fox-hunting | woods |
| churches | not many shops |
| country pubs | fishing |
| sailing | wild flowers |
| walking | horse-riding |
| pheasants | no traffic lights |
| tractors | peaceful |

## Resources needed

Notes on a topic (see 'Preparation'), board or flip chart, paper, writing materials.

## What to do

*Introduction*

Look with the children at the notes which have been made (see 'Preparation') and discuss the major points with them, emphasizing that the notes have been made quite randomly. Then show them how the notes can be sorted into a more logical order and organized into sections under appropriate headings. For example:

| farms |
|---|
| lots of farms |
| farmyard smells |
| farm animals |
| tractors |

| villages |
|---|
| small villages |
| churches |
| not many shops |
| country pubs |

| traffic |
|---|
| no traffic lights |
| narrow lanes |

| wildlife |
|---|
| pheasants |

| leisure |
|---|
| fishing |
| sailing |
| fox-hunting (this may lead to further debate) |
| walking |
| horse-riding |

| general |
|---|
| quiet |
| footpaths |
| peaceful |
| not very crowded |
| woods |
| wild flowers |

Build the notes up until the children begin to run out of ideas, then review them and look for ways of moving text around and adding headings.

### Individual/group work

Ask the children to use the notes on the board, and any other ideas which they may have, to produce a coherent piece of writing. Encourage them to make use of headings and subheadings to organize their writing.

Once the writing session is underway, stop the children occasionally to share examples of good work and to discuss any problems. Take the opportunity to write on the board any words which children experience difficulty in spelling.

Look for opportunities to review what the children have been doing and to allow them to edit and modify their work in the light of class discussions.

### Suggestion(s) for extension

Some children could work independently or in pairs to make notes based upon their reading of reference texts. Insist that they do not merely copy chunks from the books and talk with them about the importance of making concise notes which will be useful to them when they come to write in more detail.

### Suggestion(s) for support

Some children may need help with organizing their notes and turning them into prose. Work with those who experience problems and model non-fiction writing for them.

### Assessment opportunities

Look for evidence that children are able to build their notes into coherent writing and are able to make use of headings and subheadings.

### Opportunities for IT

Some children could make and sort notes using the word processor and then use these as a starting point for extended writing.

### Display ideas

Display children's original notes alongside their final drafts to illustrate the process involved, and to provide a focal point for a follow-up lesson on note-making.

### Other aspects of the English PoS covered

Reading – 2c.
Speaking and listening – 2b.

# VARYING EXPRESSION

*To reflect upon language use and to consider ways of varying expression.*

†† *Whole-class work followed by individual or paired work.*

🕐 *At least one hour.*

## Key background information

In this activity children are given a passage of information text about York which is presented in a rather dull way with an excessive number of sentences. They are asked to rewrite it, retaining all the original information. This lesson could fit into history work on Romans, Vikings, the Middle Ages or geography work on contrasting environments.

*Literacy Hour:* this activity could be done over two days, forming part of a series of Literacy Hours on varying expression. These could take place in Y5 T2 (S4) or T3 (S2) or at any stage in Y6.

## Preparation

Find some reference books or guidebooks which provide information about York. Make an enlarged copy of photocopiable 126 and multiple copies so that children may have one each or one between two.

## Resources needed

Reference books on York, photocopiable page 126, paper, writing materials.

## What to do

### Introduction

Read the text about York on photocopiable page 126 with the children, and ask them to discuss its content. Talk about the information which is given, and then ask them for their opinions on the way in which it is presented. Look at the opening paragraph and ask the children to suggest ways in which the same information could be provided in fewer sentences, and in a more interesting style. For example: *The pleasant city of York, with its old buildings and an ancient wall almost all the way round the city centre, attracts many visitors.*

Discuss the use of subordinate clauses and ways in which phrases may be combined to reduce repetition. Ask the children to think about the adjectives they use and encourage them to avoid using the same ones repeatedly.

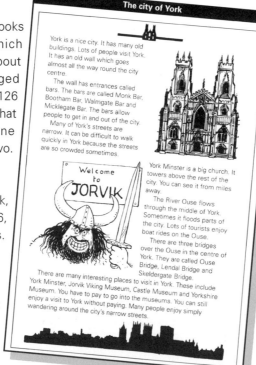

### Individual/group work

Ask the children to work individually or in pairs to rewrite the passage about York. Tell them that they must retain all the essential information, but look for ways of making it more interesting for the reader. They could do this by reducing the number of sentences; using subordinate clauses and phrases; replacing some adjectives, especially any which are repeated; and by rephrasing. Emphasize that there is no one correct way to rewrite text and that many different ways are possible.

## Suggestion(s) for extension

Children could go on to find out more about York, and could continue their writing, using an appropriate style. This would be especially useful if a visit to the city was planned. Additional material could be acquired from the Tourist Information Centre and children could write letters requesting information. They could follow this task with the rewriting of passages from guidebooks about York.

## Suggestion(s) for support

Work with a group of children to change the text on photocopiable page 126, as a shared writing activity. Draw upon the children's suggestions throughout and ask them to work independently at various points, partly so that you will be able to leave them and look at the rest of the class's work.

## Assessment opportunities

Look for evidence that children are able to construct sentences in different ways without affecting meaning.

## Opportunities for IT

Key in the text and ask the children to manipulate it using 'cut', 'paste' and 'edit'. Remember to make back-up copies of the file.

## Display ideas

Make a display on the theme of the city of York. Include the original text together with the children's versions. Add brochures and leaflets and guidebooks, as well as history books which are related to periods in York's history.

## Other aspects of the English PoS covered

Reading – 3.
Speaking and listening – 3a.

## Reference to photocopiable sheet

Photocopiable page 126 provides a non-fiction passage which is written in a repetitive style, with excessively short sentences. The children can use various techniques to rewrite it so that it is more interesting to read.

# COMPARATIVE ADJECTIVES

**To understand the different ways in which comparative and superlative adjectives may be written.**

†† *Whole-class work followed by individual or paired work.*

🕒 *At least one hour.*

## Previous skills/knowledge needed

Children will need to have discussed adjectives previously and should be aware of their functions.

## Key background information

Adjectives can be used not only to describe nouns, but also to show degrees of intensity. For example, when comparing children's height we can say that Ravi is taller than Michael and that Ravi is also the tallest person in his group. We use the suffix *-er* when comparing two people or things and *-est* when comparing more than two.

*Literacy Hour:* this lesson could form part of a series of Literacy Hours for Y4 T2 (S1) which focus on comparative adjectives. These could include work on adjectives which indicate degrees of intensity rather than measurable differences, such as *boring, interesting, exciting, thrilling.*

## Preparation

On separate cards or on the board, write a list of adjectives which relate to measurement. These could include: *tall, heavy, light, short, small, big, old, young, long, wide* and *fast.* Make some cards with the suffixes *-er* and *-est* written on them.

## Resources needed

Cards/list (see 'Preparation'), photocopiable page 127, board or flip chart, paper, writing materials.

## What to do

*Introduction*

Ask one child to come to the front and, with the help of the whole class, ascribe adjectives such as those suggested above to describe his or her measurable features. Now ask a second child to come out and ask the children to use the same adjectives to compare the two. Almost inevitably someone will suggest that one child is the tallest or the lightest. Explain that one is taller or lighter and that the suffix we use when comparing two people is *-er.*

Invite a third child to the front and ask children to use the adjectives to compare the three, explaining that we use *-est* when more than two people or things are being compared. You may wish to look at other adjectives such as *happy* and *sad,* and look at the way in which they follow the rule. Children may suggest other adjectives which do not follow the same rule, for example *good* and *cheerful.* Make a note of these on the board and add them to a display of comparative adjectives at a later date. Explain that words ending in *-ful* have to be prefaced by *more* when comparing two people and *most* when comparing more than two (*Rachel was more skilful than Sam but Alex was the most skilful*), while *good* changes to *better* and *best* (*Crewe are a good team, Barnsley are better, but Sunderland are the best*).

### Individual/group work

Ask the children to complete a copy of photocopiable page 127 in which the sentences are incomplete, but an adjective has been indicated to be included in each. Explain that the line which shows where the missing word is to be placed is the same length in every sentence and that in some cases two words will need to be used (for example *more generous, more skilful*).

Stop the class occasionally to discuss answers and to reinforce the concept of comparative and superlative adjectives.

### Suggestion(s) for extension

Ask children who finish successfully to make up their own sentences based upon the adjectives suggested in the second instruction on the photocopiable sheet.

## Suggestion(s) for support

Make a chart of adjectives showing different degrees of intensity and display it, so that those children who need support are able to use it for reference.

## Assessment opportunities

Look for evidence that children understand the different ways in which comparative and superlative adjectives may be written. You could even hold an impromptu test at the end of the lesson in which you read a succession of sentences and ask the children to choose the appropriate comparative or superlative adjective to fit into each one. For example: *Harry is taller/tallest than William. Kirsty is the older/oldest in the class. Australia were the better/best team when they played England.*

## Display ideas

Make a display of comparative and superlative adjectives and matching sentences with missing comparatives and superlatives, and ask the children to practise putting them together so that they make sense.

## Other aspects of the English PoS covered

Reading – 3.
Speaking and listening – 3a.

## Reference to photocopiable sheet

Photocopiable page 127 requires the children to complete sentences by writing in the appropriate comparative or superlative form of a given adjective. As an extension, they can create sentences including some more difficult comparatives and superlatives.

### Comparative adjectives

Name _____

Date _____

▲ Complete the sentences using the correct version of the adjectives.

Imogen is the _____ person in the class. (tall)

Mel is _____ at singing than Victoria. (good)

Ewan was _____ than Angus, but Freya was the _____ (fast)

Ben Nevis is the _____ mountain in Scotland. (high)

Ronaldo is the _____ footballer in the world. (good)

Mrs Grant had the _____ car in the whole car park. (old)

Sharifa was the _____ of four children. (young)

Salim had lots of skill but his brother, Imran, was _____ (skilful)

Mr McNamara thought his baby daughter was the _____ girl in the world. (beautiful)

The _____ river in the United States of America is the Mississippi. (long)

▲ Make up some more sentences which include the correct versions of these adjectives: *wonderful, miserable, careless, much* and *generous.* Write them on the back of the sheet.

---

# SPEECH MARKS

***To convert text from reported speech to direct speech.***

†† *Whole-class work followed by paired and individual work.*

🕐 *At least one hour.*

## Previous skills/knowledge needed

Children should have previous experience of using speech marks and should be aware of their functions. This activity could follow on from other work on dialogue which appears in the activities 'Imaginary dialogue' (see page 19) and 'Writing a script' (see page 20).

## Key background information

In this activity children are provided with a piece of text which contains reported speech but no direct speech.

Reported speech shows what is being said (speech marks are not used), while direct speech shows the actual words which are spoken (these are placed within speech marks). The children are asked to rewrite the text, incorporating dialogue and including speech marks and other appropriate punctuation for speech.

*Literacy Hour:* this lesson could be part of Literacy Hour work for Y5 T1 (S5).

## Preparation

Find some examples of reported and direct speech in books. Make an enlarged copy of photocopiable page 128 so that the first two paragraphs can be shown to the children, and make multiple copies so that each individual can work independently on the passage.

## Resources needed

Examples of reported and direct speech from books, photocopiable page 128, paper, writing materials.

## What to do

### Introduction

Give out copies of photocopiable page 128. Read the text with the whole class and discuss its content and any unfamiliar words and phrases.

Now read the opening two paragraphs and ask the children if they could write them in a different way so that the reader knows the exact words that the girls speak. Ask some children to take the parts of Sarah and Rebecca and to say the words which they think the girls might have spoken.

Discuss the use of speech marks (you may wish to mention that double and single speech marks are equally acceptable so long as they are used consistently) and show the children how the dialogue could be written. For example:

The two friends looked at each other. 'I've never been so afraid,' said Sarah.
'Neither have I,' agreed Rebecca.
'Don't worry, Rebecca,' said Sarah comfortingly. 'Here, have a piece of chocolate to keep your spirits up.'

### Individual/group work

Ask the children to work in pairs to change the text into direct speech. Encourage them to record, within speech marks, the exact words which they think each character would have said. Tell them that they will need to make it clear who is speaking, and that they should also include other background information which appears in the text. When they have completed the work successfully they should be able to read the speech alone, taking the parts of the characters, and it should sound like a conversation.

### Suggestion(s) for extension

Some children could write further dialogue for the 'journey home' narrative.

### Suggestion(s) for support

Encourage the children to do the activity orally before writing anything down. Work with them to read the text,

and then ascribe a role to each child and invite them to work out which words the characters would actually have spoken. Write the dialogue with them as a shared writing exercise, until they feel confident to attempt it in pairs.

### Assessment opportunities

Look for evidence that children are able to punctuate speech accurately.

### Opportunities for IT

Present the text as a file for children to use 'cut', 'paste' and 'edit' to change it into direct speech. Make sure you make back-up copies so that this can be repeated.

### Display ideas

Display examples of direct and indirect speech together with the photocopiable sheet and some examples of the ways in which the children rewrote the text for the activity. At the centre of the display, place an enlarged written exchange between two characters to illustrate the correct punctuation for direct speech.

### Other aspects of the English PoS covered

Reading – 3.
Speaking and listening – 3a.

### Reference to photocopiable sheet

Photocopiable page 128 provides a short story which includes reported speech; the children change the text so that only direct speech is used.

The broken window, see page 13

# The broken window: part one

There was a horrible moment when every breath was held as the ball sped towards the staffroom window, then there was a shattering, crashing sound as the glass exploded into a thousand pieces.

The players stopped. Everyone in the playground fell silent and there was an awful hush before a loud, stern adult voice broke the silence. "Who on earth is responsible for this?"

Miss Carmichael's red and angry face appeared at the smashed staffroom window and her eyes scanned the playground. "Come along, I want to know who broke this window immediately, if not sooner!"

The playground remained silent and still for a few seconds longer and then Jessica stepped forward and raised her hand. "I'm sorry Miss, it was me," she said in a voice which trembled with fear.

"You, Jessica Scott, you? You kicked a ball so hard that it smashed the staffroom window? Go and stand outside my office and wait for me there!"

As Jessica trudged from the playground, the other children stood silently watching her. She was near to tears as she feared the punishment that Miss Carmichael might give to her. She had read stories in which children at private schools were given hundreds of lines to write or were made to pick up litter for a week. She had even read of children being beaten. As she trooped across the playground, she thought of running away and going back to the house at Little Rowton – she would wait until dark before climbing back through the trapdoor into her bedroom, and leaving this place for ever.

Her thoughts were interrupted by the sound of clapping. She looked up and through her already tear-stained eyes she saw that one by one, and

The broken window, see page 13

## The broken window: part one (cont.)

then all together, the other children were applauding her. "Great shot, Scotty!" called Kenneth, and the others joined in with similar cries. Amanda ran to her and put an arm around her shoulders. "Don't worry, Jessica," she said, "it won't be all that bad."

Jessica didn't know whether to be happy about the reaction of the others or terrified about the action that Miss Carmichael might take. The headteacher had been friendly when she had called her into her office the day before, but now she sounded angry and fierce. Jessica climbed the stairs to the office as slowly as if she were about to have a tooth out at the dentist's. There was no chair outside Miss Carmichael's room, so she stood uncomfortably, hopping from foot to foot, thinking about the dreadful punishment that she might be given.

After what seemed an hour, but what was probably only about five minutes, Miss Carmichael's footsteps could be heard coming up the stairs getting louder and more menacing as they neared her office. Jessica hardly dared to look at her as she reached the end of the corridor. "Well may you avoid my eyes, young lady!" thundered Miss Carmichael in a voice which confirmed Jessica's worst fears. "Go into my office!"

Jessica could hardly turn the doorknob, her hands were shaking so much. After a few moments of fumbling she managed to open the door and entered the room followed by the headteacher.

FURTHER *Curriculum Bank* ACTIVITIES
**PHOTOCOPIABLES**

Girls don't play football, see page 15

# The broken window: part two

"Now, Miss Scott, what have you to say for yourself?"

"I-I-I'm sorry, Miss," stammered the miserable looking girl. "I-I didn't mean to break the window. I was just playing football and…"

"You were playing football! Why were you playing football? Girls don't play football!"

Despite her fear of punishment, Jessica could not let Miss Carmichael's words pass. "Yes they do, Miss. There are women's teams and in Italy women can be professionals and anyway they've got just as much right to play football as boys." She heard her voice becoming louder as she continued. "Boys play hockey and no one complains about that…" Before she could continue Miss Carmichael interrupted her.

"Excellent reply, my dear. Jolly well done!"

Jessica was almost as confused as she had been when she first went through the trapdoor which had led her to this place. She had broken a window. She had just raised her voice to the headteacher. She was expecting a terrible punishment and Miss Carmichael had just congratulated her on what she had said.

"Jolly well done, Miss?"

"Yes, Jessica, jolly well done! Sit down please. I want to talk to you."

Jessica did as she was told and sat in the same chair that she had occupied last time she had been in the Head's office.

"Actually, Mr Green has already told me about your footballing talents, so it was no surprise to find that it was you who broke the window. Tell me, my dear, did you score?"

"Yes, Miss, but I never meant to break the window, honestly." Jessica was still not certain that she would not be punished.

"Of course you didn't, my dear. No one but an idiot would break a window on

Girls don't play football, see page 15

## The broken window: part two (cont.)

purpose. Unfortunately, we do have one or two idiots in this school so I had to raise my voice for their benefit. I do hope that I didn't frighten you."

Jessica admitted that she had been terrified.

"Well, there's no need to be," said Miss Carmichael with smiling eyes. "You should be proud of yourself. Far too many girls of your age don't stand up for themselves. They believe it when boys and even some girls tell them that they can't play football. Well, as far as I'm concerned football is a game for anyone who wants to play it. Between you and me, I've been meaning to do something about those games lessons where the boys play one game while the girls play another for some time. I thought there would be lots of objections, but after what you have done with a football in the last two days I think most people will agree to a few changes, don't you?"

Jessica was too bewildered to answer.

"Now, if I'm going to be able to convince everyone, I need your help, Jessica. Will you help me?" The teacher's voice was now gentle and friendly and quite unlike the booming tones which had echoed across the playground only a few minutes earlier.

Dear Jack, see page 17

# Dear Jack...

The Castle
Stalk Top
FEF1 F0

21 October

Dear Jack

As you probably know, I have been very tired lately. It is hard work looking after the whole castle and my wife is not as young as she used to be.

I have been trying to save the golden eggs the goose lays, so that I can sell them and be able to afford to pay someone to come and cook and clean for us. Unfortunately, every time I come down the beanstalk and go to the bank, everyone runs away screaming. Another problem is that I am too big to get through the door of the bank!

I expect you were pretty frightened the other day when I woke up and chased you and I don't blame you for chopping the beanstalk down. The castle was quite badly damaged, so my wife and I have decided to move to another area and set up home there.

Anyway, I'm sorry I was so cross and I honestly would never have hurt you, but I wonder if you would do me a great favour. You see, we need some money to build a house and now that you have taken our golden goose, we just don't have any. Do you think you could lend me the goose for a few days so that it could lay some golden eggs for us? I would give the goose back to you as soon as I had finished, honestly. There is a bank near here where I think they would exchange the eggs for cash. I went the other day and the manager said he would do anything for me as long as I didn't hurt him.

Please write back and tell me that you will help us. It will soon be winter and I really feel the cold.

Best wishes

Giant

Imaginary dialogue, see page 19

# Goldilocks and Cinderella in conversation (1)

"So go on, tell me about this fairy godmother of yours," said Goldilocks.

Well, it was strange really," said Cinderella. "One minute I was scrubbing the kitchen floor and keeping an eye on a pan full of porridge, and the next I was looking at this peculiar old lady who was wearing a silver dress and carrying a magic wand."

"Porridge, eh?" said Goldilocks. "I'm rather fond of porridge."

"Look, do you want to hear my story or not?" asked Cinderella huffily.

"Of course I do," replied Goldilocks. "I'm sorry, but I had rather a nasty experience the other day."

"Well tell me about it later. It's my turn now!" said Cinderella crossly. "Now where was I?"

"You had just met a lady in a silver dress who carried a magic wand," prompted Goldilocks.

"Ah yes. Well she just looked at me kneeling on the floor surrounded by soap suds and she smelled the porridge on the stove and she asked me if I needed a night out."

"And what did you say?"

"I told her that would be wonderful and I asked her if she was going to scrub the floor and make the porridge while I went to a disco. 'Oh no,' she said, 'I don't scrub floors. I do magic!'"

"What happened?" asked Goldilocks eagerly.

"Well she just sort of waved her wand and suddenly I was wearing a beautiful dress and the floor was clean and the porridge had disappeared. Then she told me to go to the window and, as I did, she waved her wand again and turned mice and pumpkins into a coach and horses. I don't mind telling you, I was speechless."

"That would make a change!" laughed Goldilocks.

"Look, if you're going to be cheeky, I'm not going to tell you any more," grumbled Cinderella.

"I'm sorry," said Goldilocks, "please carry on."

Writing a script, see page 20

## Goldilocks and Cinderella in conversation (2)

GOLDILOCKS:  So go on, tell me about this fairy godmother of yours.

CINDERELLA:  Well, it was strange really. One minute I was scrubbing the kitchen floor and keeping an eye on a pan full of porridge and the next I was looking at this peculiar old lady who was wearing a silver dress and carrying a magic wand.

GOLDILOCKS:  Porridge, eh? I'm rather fond of porridge.

CINDERELLA:  Look do you want to hear my story or not?

GOLDILOCKS:  Of course I do. I'm sorry, but I had rather a nasty experience the other day.

CINDERELLA:  *(impatiently)* Well tell me about it later. It's my turn now! Now where was I?

GOLDILOCKS:  You had just met a lady in a silver dress who carried a magic wand.

CINDERELLA:  Ah yes. Well she just looked at me kneeling on the floor surrounded by soap suds and she smelled the porridge on the stove and she asked me if I needed a night out.

GOLDILOCKS:  And what did you say?

CINDERELLA:  I told her that would be wonderful and I asked her if she was going to scrub the floor and make the porridge while I went to a disco. "Oh no," she said, "I don't scrub floors. I do magic!"

GOLDILOCKS:  What happened?

CINDERELLA:  Well she just sort of waved her wand and suddenly I was wearing a beautiful dress and the floor was clean and the porridge had disappeared. Then she told me to go to the window and, as I did, she waved her wand again and turned mice and pumpkins into a coach and horses. I don't mind telling you, I was speechless.

GOLDILOCKS:  *(laughing)* That would make a change!

CINDERELLA:  *(crossly)* Look, if you're going to be cheeky, I'm not going to tell you any more.

GOLDILOCKS:  I'm sorry, please carry on.

My best friend, see page 23

# A best friend

Name _____     Date _____

The things I like most about my best friend are: _____

_____

_____

_____

My best friend always: _____

_____

_____

My best friend never: _____

_____

_____

The nicest thing my best friend ever did was: _____

_____

_____

_____

The worst thing my best friend ever did was: _____

_____

_____

My best friend's best quality is: _____

_____

_____

_____

_____

_____

_____

_____

My best friend

# Another planet

There was an air of trepidation in the cockpit as we descended slowly towards the planet which we had always called Zuron. The three of us, Mike, Becky and myself, looked at each other anxiously as we peered out of the hatches and saw the land appearing to rise towards us.

This was a new experience for all of us. Our previous voyages had taken us to known parts of the Solar System. We had only ever visited planets which had been visited before by people from Earth. This time it was different. We would be the first humans to set foot on Zuron. We looked down at the dry, barren land. Becky, the expert on other life forms, looked both anxious and excited. She desperately wanted to find signs of life but, like the rest of us, she was afraid that we might find enemies if we discovered anything.

Mike fired the remaining retro rockets and our descent slowed as the dust from the ground cascaded into the air blocking our view. Suddenly, with a thud and a rattle, we landed. The space module rocked alarmingly and then settled. Everything was still and quiet.

We looked through the hatches to see if the planet contained anything more interesting than rocks and sand. Each of our mouths fell open in unison and there was a collective gasp as a picture emerged through the settling dust.

Bill's New Frock, see page 26

# Boys and girls/girls and boys

Name _____     Date _____

|  | Boys | Girls |
|---|---|---|
| On the way to school |  |  |
| In the playground |  |  |
| In lessons |  |  |
| At lunchtime |  |  |
| At home |  |  |

Flannan Isle, see page 27

# Flannan Isle

*"Though three men dwell on Flannan Isle*
*To keep the lamp alight,*
*As we steered under the lee, we caught*
*No glimmer through the night."*

A passing ship at dawn had brought
The news, and quickly we set sail,
To find out what strange thing might ail
The keepers of the deep-sea light.

The winter day broke blue and bright
With glancing sun and glancing spray
While o'er the swell our boat made way,
As gallant as a gull in flight.

But as we neared the lonely Isle
And looked up at the naked height,
And saw the lighthouse towering white
With blinded lantern, that all night
Had never shot a spark
Of comfort through the dark,
So ghostly in the cold sunlight
It seemed that we were struck the while
With wonder all too dread for words.

And, as into the tiny creek
We stole beneath the hanging crag,
We saw three queer black ugly birds –
Too big by far in my belief,
For cormorant or shag –
Like seamen sitting bolt-upright

Up on a half-tide reef:
But, as we neared, they plunged from sight
Without a sound or spurt of white.

And still too mazed to speak,
We landed; and made fast the boat;
And climbed the track in single file,
Each wishing he was safe afloat
On any sea, however far,
So it be far from Flannan Isle:
And still we seemed to climb and climb
As though we'd lost all count of time
And so must climb for evermore.
Yet, all too soon, we reached the door –
The black, sun-blistered lighthouse-door,
That gaped for us ajar.

As, on the threshold, for a spell
We paused, we seemed to breathe the smell
Of limewash and of tar,
Familiar as our daily breath,
As though 'twere some strange scent of death;
And so yet wondering, side by side
We stood a moment still tongue-tied;
And each with black foreboding eyed
The door, ere we should fling it wide
To leave the sunlight for the gloom:
Till, plucking courage up, at last
Hard on each other's heels we passed
Into the living-room.

Flannan Isle, see page 27

# Flannan Isle (cont.)

Yet, as we crowded through the door
We only saw a table, spread
For dinner, meat and cheese and bread;
But all untouched; and no one there:
As though, when they sat down to eat,
Ere they could even taste,
Alarm had come; and they in haste
Had risen and left the bread and meat,
For at the table-head a chair
Lay tumbled on the floor.

We listened, but we only heard
The feeble chirping of a bird
That starved upon its perch;
And listening still, without a word
We set about our hopeless search.
We hunted high, we hunted low,
And soon ransacked the empty house;
Then o'er the Island, to and fro
We ranged to listen and to look
In every cranny, cleft or nook
That might have hid a bird or mouse:
But though we searched from shore to shore
We found no sign in any place,
And soon again stood face to face
Before the gaping door,
And stole into the room once more
As frightened children steal.

Ay, though we hunted high and low
And hunted everywhere,
Of the three men's fate we found no trace
Of any kind in any place
but a door ajar, and an untouched meal,
And an overtoppled chair.

And as we listened in the gloom
Of that forsaken living-room –
A chill clutch on our breath –
We thought how ill-chance came to all
Who kept the Flannan Light,
And how the rock had been the death
Of many a likely lad –
How six had come to a sudden end
And three had gone stark mad,
And one whom we'd all known as friend
Had leapt from the lantern one still night,
And fallen dead by the lighthouse wall –
And long we thought
On the three we sought,
And on what might yet befall.

Like curs a glance has brought to heel
We listened, flinching there,
And looked, and looked, on the untouched meal,
And the overtoppled chair.

We seemed to stand for an endless while,
Though still no word was said,
Three men alive on Flannan Isle
Who thought on three men dead.

*Wilfred Wilson Gibson*

# Jessica's other house

It was on a dark, foggy March night when Jessica was lying awake listening to her sister Emma's snoring that her adventure began. Her legs hung over the edge of the bed because her sisters had taken up most of the room, and she was cold and uncomfortable. The bed was old and had long legs which raised it nearly a metre off the floor. Jessica decided that she would wrap herself in the spare blanket and try to sleep under the bed. The springs creaked as she crept out of bed, but her sisters hardly stirred. As quietly as she could, Jessica slid under the bed and rolled herself up in a rather musty smelling blanket.

The floor was hard and bare and the floorboards smelled of ancient varnish. She closed her eyes and tried counting sheep. She had just managed to visualize dozens of the woolly creatures leaping one by one through a gap in a hawthorn hedge, when she felt something sticking into her back. She felt around on the floor and found what seemed like a large ring. Rolling over, Jessica tried to pick up the ring but it was attached to the floor. She noticed though that the floor seemed to lift a little as she tugged.

Jessica was now wide awake and she was curious. Next to the bed, on Jane's side, was a small torch which the girls used to read under the blankets when their mother told them to put the light out. Jessica crawled under the bed until she came out next to Jane and she reached for the torch. It was too dark to see anything and, just as she put her hand out to pick the torch up from the bedside table, she lost her grip and the torch clattered to the floor. She froze. Her sisters stirred and Emma coughed, but then the girls quickly settled back to their rhythmic breathing and snoring.

The little girl reached her hand along the floor until she felt the torch and she carefully picked it up. Under the bed, she shone the torch around until it lighted the area where she had been lying. There *was* a ring. It was about six centimetres in diameter and it was fixed to the floor. Jessica looked more closely and saw that there was a  narrow gap in the floorboards near to the ring and that this formed a square of perhaps half a metre in width. She had never looked under the bed so closely before and she suspected that no one else had either. When the girls tidied their room, they usually threw everything under the bed and forgot about it. She could certainly never remember the bed being moved.

Jessica took the ring in her hands and pulled. The floorboards creaked slightly and a square of floor lifted. She only raised it a little, but as she did so she noticed a bright light shining from three sides of the square. It was difficult to

100

# Jessica's other house (cont.)

find enough room under the bed to pull at the ring properly and she had to lie on her side. Even then, she kept bumping her head on the springs and she was afraid that she would wake her sisters. Finally, she managed to lift the boards enough to slide a slipper into the gap to prop them up. Once she had done this, it was possible to slide the wood away from its position. She took the ring in both hands and rolled away onto her back. As she did so, the wood moved and the underside of the bed was suddenly illuminated.

Jessica rolled back and saw that a square of light had been revealed. She turned onto her stomach and peered into it. She had expected that the hole would contain a light. How else could she explain the brightness which had come from it? She was surprised by what she did see. In fact, she could hardly believe her eyes. A ladder led from what she now knew to be a hatch down to a carpeted floor. She could see a wall with pictures on it and a large clock which she could hear ticking.

Jessica knew she would have to descend the ladder to find out more about the room below. She had never seen this part of her house before and she could hardly believe that it could exist without her knowing about it. After all, the house was tiny with only two rooms upstairs and a living room, bathroom and a kitchen downstairs. There was no space for anything else.

The ladder was metal and it felt cold on her bare feet. Once, as she carefully climbed down, she caught her foot in her nightie and almost fell, but she managed to reach the carpeted floor safely and she looked around her in amazement. The first thing she noticed was that she was not in a room at all, but on a landing. Several doors opened off it and at the end there was a wide staircase with polished wooden banisters. The carpet was thick and warm. In fact, the whole place felt much warmer than the chilly bedroom that she had left.

Suddenly, she heard a voice. "What are you doing here?" it asked.

# Triolets

Name _____    Date _____

▲ Complete the triolets and then try writing some of your own.

_____    _____ really hates,

Anyone who hits his mates.

_____

_____    _____ really hates,

_____

He's quite a fussy creature.

_____    _____ really hates,

Anyone who hits his mates.

———◄●►———

Whenever things go wrong, it's always Steve,
He gets in trouble you would not believe,

_____

Whenever things go wrong, it's always Steve.

_____

_____

Whenever things go wrong, it's always Steve,
He gets in trouble you would not believe.

———◄●►———

Sophie Spooner couldn't help but sneeze,

_____

Sophie Spooner couldn't help but sneeze,

_____

_____

Sophie Spooner couldn't help but sneeze,

_____

WRITING KEY STAGE TWO

Character sketches, see page 39

# Character sketches

## *Jim Baker*

Jim Baker was one of the most evil pirates ever to sail the seas. His face was set in an almost permanent scowl and he only ever smiled when he was ordering his enemies to walk the plank.

Baker led a band of vicious cut-throats for seven years, and they terrorized honest sailors in every part of the globe. The pirates robbed ships of their cargoes and attacked their crews, and made themselves fabulously rich in the process. Often, Baker left the unfortunate sailors on deserted islands where they had little hope of being rescued.

Baker did not even care for animals and never possessed a parrot as some pirates did. His only pet was a snarling mongrel dog which he treated so terribly that it frequently bit strangers.

Baker's features were unmistakable. On his left cheek was a long scar, which he got when boarding a French ship with his cut-throat band to steal food which was bound for Spain. His right eye was covered with a black patch, not because there was anything wrong with it, but because he thought the patch made him look more fearsome.

Jim Baker died in 1763 when he fell into the English Channel while attacking a hospital ship. He will long be remembered, but he was missed by few.

## *Joan Dix*

Joan Dix is one of the kindest people you could wish to meet. Nothing is ever too much trouble for her and she is very popular with everyone in her village.

When people are ill, she is always the first to visit them and take them flowers or grapes. If someone is too old to go to the shops, she will often walk all the way to the nearest town, which is five miles away, to fetch shopping, and she often deliberately 'forgets' to ask them for the money to pay for the goods.

When she was a girl, Joan saved her baby brother's life by going into a burning house and bringing him out after the Fire Brigade had given up all hope of saving him. She suffered burns to her face which can still be seen, but she never tries to hide them and doesn't seem to mind when people stare at her.

Someone in the village once said that if Joan had never been born, someone would have had to invent her. No one could imagine what life would be like without her.

# Interpreting charts

| Child's name | Age | Height | Weight | Time taken to run 50 metres |
|---|---|---|---|---|
| Grace | 9Y 4M | 135cm | 31kg | 10 seconds |
| Milo | 10Y 6M | 152cm | 33kg | 11 seconds |
| Naseem | 8Y 3M | 143cm | 29kg | 12 seconds |
| Tom | 6Y 8M | 136cm | 24kg | 22 seconds |
| Helen | 7Y 2M | 129cm | 26kg | 20 seconds |

# Two match reports

## BARNSLEY WIN BY BIG SCORE

*Barnsley 7   Huddersfield Town 1*

Last night at Oakwell, Barnsley scored six goals in the first half of their match against Huddersfield. This was Barnsley's best performance of the season and the crowd of 16,648 went home very happy.

Bruce Dyer scored the first goal in the tenth minute, then Craig Hignett scored two goals. Eric Tinkler scored Barnsley's fourth goal and then Ashley Ward scored another. The best goal of the night was scored by Darren Barnard with a shot from twenty metres.

In the second half, Huddersfield fought hard but Barnsley missed a penalty and then Bruce Dyer scored the home team's seventh goal. Delroy Facey scored for Huddersfield after 74 minutes, but it was too late for them to have any chance of saving the game.

## SUPER REDS SHATTER TOWN

*Barnsley 7   Huddersfield Town 1*

In one of the most memorable games seen at Oakwell for years, Barnsley last night produced a blistering first half performance which swept aside their Yorkshire rivals and delighted most of the 16,000 crowd.

Huddersfield were simply overwhelmed, as goals from Dyer, Hignett (2), Tinkler and Ward gave Barnsley a five-goal lead after only 37 minutes. The home supporters thought things could not get any better, but they did after 40 minutes when Darren Barnard thundered Nicky Eaden's cross into the net from twenty

metres. There was a moment's pause as the stunned crowd held their breath in disbelief, before Oakwell erupted into celebrations of the best goal seen on the ground in living memory.

The second half was something of an anticlimax, but Barnsley continued to dominate, despite a brave fightback by the visitors for whom Facey scored a consolation goal in the 74th minute. By that time, however, Barnsley had scored again through Dyer, who had a splendid match, and even missed a penalty when Hignett blasted the ball over the bar after Ward had been fouled.

## Letter to a councillor

24 November 2000

Councillor Edna Welthorpe
Borchester Town Hall
BORCHESTER  BR1 3AT

Dear Councillor Welthorpe

I am writing to ask for your help in improving our local park.

   As you may know, King George's Park has been used by the people of Brinkley for over one hundred years. However, recently the park has become less popular because many of the facilities have been vandalized.

   The swings, slide and roundabouts have been broken and litter bins have been tipped up. Some people even pick flowers from the flowerbeds and others let their dogs make messes on the playing fields. As a result, a lot of people no longer go to the park and I think this is very sad.

   I would like to suggest that the Council should employ an extra park keeper to patrol the park and try to catch the people who are spoiling it for everyone else. I also think that money should be spent on improving the children's playground and repairing the broken items. I am sure that if the park looked nice again and if the vandals knew they would be caught if they damaged it, people would start visiting it again. The council could even make enough money to pay for the repairs and the park keeper, if it opened an ice-cream stall and a café.

   I do hope that you will think about my suggestions and that you will help to make King George's Park into a good place to visit once again.

Yours sincerely

*Kate Downing*

Kate Downing

The town (1) and (3), see pages 57 and 60

# Town plan

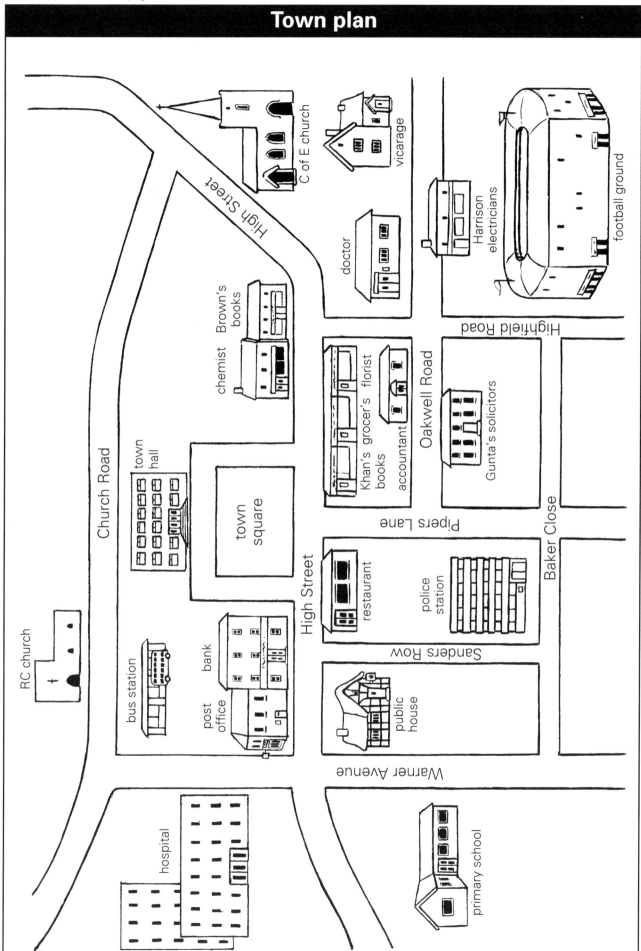

The town (1), see page 57

# Residents of the town

✂

| | | | |
|---|---|---|---|
| Mr Jones<br>*road-sweeper* | Mr Williams<br>*nurse* | Mrs Firn<br>*florist* | Miss King<br>*supermarket manager* |
| Mrs Jones<br>*shop assistant at Brown's Bookshop* | Michael Williams<br>*pupil at primary school* | Mr Harrison<br>*electrician* | Mr Turner<br>*butcher* |
| Mr Morton<br>*traffic warden* | Daniel Harrison<br>*pupil at primary school* | Mrs Lewis<br>*bank manager* | Mrs Turner<br>*newsagent* |
| Sally Morton<br>Mr Morton's daughter, *doctor* | Amy Lewis<br>*pupil at primary school* | Mrs Barker<br>*bank clerk* | Kylie Turner<br>*pupil at secondary school* |
| Miss Charlton<br>*headteacher of primary school* | Usha Gunta<br>*pupil at primary school* | Devon Hartley<br>*professional footballer* | Mr Wilson<br>*landlord of public house* |
| Mr Smith<br>*teacher at primary school* | Mrs Gunta<br>*solicitor* | Lee Winters<br>*apprentice electrician* | Mr Robson<br>*postman* |
| Mr Thomas<br>*chemist* | Mr Gunta<br>*accountant* | Mrs Garton<br>*pensioner* | Mrs Robson<br>*chef at restaurant* |
| Mrs Thomas<br>*mayor* | Miss Davis<br>*bus driver* | Revd. Morris<br>*vicar* | Father O'Riley<br>*priest* |
| Mrs Williams<br>*police officer* | Mr Firn<br>*greengrocer* | Mr Norton<br>*plumber* | Mrs Khan<br>*bookshop owner* |

Vocabulary extension (1), see page 62

## Adverbs

Name _____    Date _____

▲ Add adverbs where you think they are needed.

**The Escape**

The light was fading. I ran down the road. My heart was beating. In the distance

I could see my house. Behind me, the footsteps were still pounding. I was

puffing and panting, but I knew that I had to keep running if I was to escape.

   I looked around. I could see no one, but I knew that they were there. Once

again, I ran. Once again, I heard the footsteps.

   The house was visible and I could see the light in the kitchen, but it might as

well have been a hundred kilometres away. I just didn't think I could reach it

before they caught up with me.


▲ Would you change any of the adverbs in this version of the story?

**The Escape**

The light was fading rapidly. I ran wearily down the road. My heart was beating
fast. In the distance I could clearly see my house. Behind me, the footsteps
were still pounding loudly. I was puffing and panting heavily, but I knew that I
had to keep running quickly if I was to escape.
   I looked around cautiously. I could see no one, but I certainly knew that they
were there. Once again, I ran quickly. Once again, I clearly heard the footsteps.
   The house was clearly visible and I could definitely see the light in the
kitchen, but it might as well have been a hundred kilometres away. I just didn't
think I could reach it safely before they caught up with me.

Vocabulary extension (2), see page 64

# On the beach

Name _____          Date _____

▲ Can you make this passage more interesting?

The sun was hot and the sky was blue, as we ran down to the sandy beach.

We could hardly wait to paddle in the wet sea and make castles with the dry

sand. I had a red spade and a green bucket and Saffi carried a yellow ball.

We were going to have a great time.

   As we reached the beach, we dropped our things onto the dry sand and

quickly put on our new swimming things. I had white trunks and Saffi had a

black costume. The sandy beach was almost deserted, as we ran towards the

blue sea.

| **Sample adjectives** |
| --- |
| powdery |
| golden |
| warm |
| metal |
| clear |
| plastic |
| bright |
| salty |
| inviting |

Plurals (1), see page 65

# Singulars and plurals (1)

Name _____    Date _____

▲ Match the plural words to the singular words.

| monkey | key | dish | baby | knife |

| fish | child | mouse | roof |

| fox | sheep | foot |

| man | tooth |

---

| roofs | fish/fishes |

| sheep | dishes | babies |

| feet | foxes | keys | men |

| children | monkeys | teeth | knives | mice |

Plurals (1), see page 65

# Singulars and plurals in sentences

Name _____  Date _____

▲ Rewrite the sentences so that the underlined words are plurals. Look carefully to see if you need to change any other words so that the sentences make sense.

Ashley jumped in the air after he scored a <u>goal</u>.

_____

The <u>bus</u> was late as usual.

_____

My pet <u>dog</u> is full of fun.

_____

Nicky's <u>foot</u> was aching after the long walk home.

_____

The small <u>child</u> was looking out of the <u>window</u> longing for it to stop raining.

_____

The <u>girl</u> is sitting on a sofa.

_____

The <u>dog</u> wagged its tail.

_____

Nasser's <u>tooth</u> was loose and it was about to fall out.

_____

Plurals (2), see page 67

# Singulars and plurals (2)

Name _____    Date _____

▲ Change the underlined words from singular to plural. Look carefully to see if you need to change any other words too.

The <u>squirrel</u> hid its acorns in a <u>hole</u> in the <u>tree</u> and scampered along the <u>branch</u>.

His back brushed against a <u>leaf</u> as he dashed off to find more food. He was

getting ready for winter.

   Beneath the <u>tree</u> a <u>fox</u> hunted for something to eat. He eyed the <u>squirrel</u> with

interest. The weather was changing and it would not be long before the first

frost. <u>He</u> needed to find food for his <u>family</u>.

   The hedge around the field was losing its leaves. A red <u>berry</u> lay on the

ground beneath it. The <u>fox</u> had eaten

fruit before when he had been really

hungry, but he preferred meat.

   Suddenly, the sky was lit up by a

<u>flash</u> of lightning. A startled <u>thrush</u>,

which had been hunting for snails

nearby, flew into the air as the first

<u>echo</u> of thunder was heard.

Subordinate clauses and phrases, see page 68

# · Using subordinate clauses and phrases

Name _____  Date _____

▲ Rewrite the pairs of sentences as single sentences.

Sally had a pet cat. Sally loved animals.

_____

Ian broke his ankle. Ian loved playing rugby.

_____

Faizal was a brilliant swimmer. Faizal had a new pair of goggles.

_____

Eric made people laugh. Eric was a comedian from Morecambe.

_____

Oscar was always using his computer. He owned lots of computer games.

_____

_____

Rachel loved climbing trees. She was always coming home with dirty clothes.

_____

_____

The dog was called Toby. He loved chasing cats.

_____

Daisy is a very intelligent girl. Daisy's best friend is Geeta.

_____

Subordinate clauses and phrases, see page 68

# Matching the subordinates to the main sentences

Name _____     Date _____

▲ Read the sentences and then choose a clause from the box to add to each one. Write the new sentences.

Tom played for the school team.

_____

_____

Sara read a book about medicines.

_____

_____

Raj went to the dentist.

_____

_____

Ruth looked after the cows.

_____

_____

Ben ate two plates of fish and chips.

_____

_____

| who had terrible toothache | who was really hungry |

| who could kick the ball harder than anyone in his class |

| who loved animals | whose mother was a doctor |

▲ Can you make up some of your own subordinate clauses and phrases to add to the sentences? Write them on the back of the sheet.

Past tense, see page 70

# A day in Oxford

Name _____     Date _____

▲ Rewrite this passage in the box, using the past tense.

On Saturdays we go to Oxford. We travel by car and park at the Park and Ride car park. We take the bus into the centre of the city.

In the morning we watch the street performers and go shopping. We have a drink in a café and my sister and I have a doughnut.

We have pizza for lunch. That is my favourite part of the day.

In the afternoon my dad and I go to watch a football match, while my mum and my sister visit the museums and go to the shops.

We all meet up in a café after the match and have a cup of tea. Then we catch the bus back to the car park and get into the car and drive home.

Verb exchange, see page 71

## Replace the verbs

Name _____  Date _____

▲ Identify the verbs in the sentences and then replace them with different verbs.

Peter walked down the road.

_____

_____

Jane climbed over a fence.

_____

Sasha laughed when she heard the joke.

_____

Ali kicked the ball into the goal as the crowd cheered.

_____

_____

Lewis threw the ball to Megan and she caught it.

_____

Kate giggled as she dropped her dinner on to the floor.

_____

_____

The rain poured from the dark clouds and the wind blew strongly.

_____

_____

Matthew is one of the cleverest children in the class at using a computer but he is hopeless at tidying his room.

_____

_____

Proofreading, see page 73

# Check this out

Name _____     Date _____

▲ Read the paragraphs and then use the checklist to help you to check them.
Mark mistakes with a coloured pen.

simon was always grumbling. he grumbled if the whether was to hot and he
grumbled if it was too cold simon's friend, daniel, was always telling simon to
stop complaining but simon tuck no notice

   one suny july day the too freinds were playing cricket when daniel hit the ball
into a garden Their was a terrible crashing sownd and the boys new that the ball
had broken a window Thay ran to the garden fence and lucked over it. mr jones,
who owned the garden, wos standing next to his grean house looking very
cross. There was a hole in one of the windows and simon could see broken
glass all over mr jones' tomartoe plants.

   "hoo did this?" said mr jones angrily. "Wos it you two?"

   daniel and simon looked at each other and the simon spoke.

   "yes, we did it but we're not sorry. I've just come round to complane. you
really shouldn't build a greanhouse so near to the playing feeld. i bet our ball has
bean damaged by all that broken glass!"

   daniel hid his eyes. he could not beleave what simon had just sed. when he
looked at mr jones he could tel that simon had said the rong thing. mr jones
face was as red as one of his toamtoes and daniel wood not have bean
surprised if steam had come out of mr jones ears.

---

CHECKLIST
• Does every sentence begin with a capital letter?
• Does every paragraph begin with a capital letter?
• Does every sentence end with a full stop or a
question mark or an exclamation mark?
• Do all special names begin with capital letters?
• Are there some words which you are sure are
spelled incorrectly? Change them.
• Are there some words which you think may be
spelled incorrectly? Check them using a dictionary.

Confusing sentences, see page 74

# Confusing sentences

▲ Can you tell what the sentences tell us in their present form? Can you rewrite them so that they make more sense?

"I'm looking for a really good girl's coat," said Caitlin.

Ryan pushed Bill in his kitchen.

Mr Aldridge spent two hours shooting at his farm.

Kyle was going to pass the ball but decided to shoot himself instead.

Saffi hid from her sister in her favourite jumper.

Mrs Murphy sailed to the Isle of Man in a blue dress.

Sam taught his dog to do tricks better than his father.

Hayley had a third child called Edward.

The boxer was a tall man with a broken nose called Henry.

Helping himself to a cake, Kieran walked to the door and popped it in his mouth.

Alistair opened the door in his pyjamas.

Simple English, see page 76

## Simple English

Name _____     Date _____

▲ Rewrite the sentences concisely.

I myself personally think that it is not unlikely that rain will fall tomorrow.

_____

At this present moment in time we have an ongoing period of sunshine.

_____

Both of the two twins wore red jumpers.

_____

Each and every person in the class had to stay in at playtime.

_____

Sasha has got a new bicycle and Daniel has got one too.

_____

"I have not got any money," said Tim.

_____

In spite of the fact that it was raining, Ruth had not got her hat on.

_____

On the day before this one the sun shone in the sky.

_____

In the month which comes between March and May the weather began to change for the better.

_____

Apostrophes, see page 78

# Apostrophes

Name _____     Date _____

▲ In this passage, some apostrophes are missing, some are in the wrong places and some shouldn't be there at all. Can you correct it?

Apostrophes can be found in all sorts of place's. It's not unusual to see apostrophes being used in plural's, especially at greengrocer's shops. You often find that carrot's, bean's, cabbage's and pea's are on sale. Perhaps the people who write such things think that the words look better with apostrophes!

Some people cant understand why we need to bother to use apostrophe's and so they miss them out altogether. However, apostrophes' can be very useful and can help us to understand meaning's. For instance, in the sentence below the apostrophe tells us how many people owned the dog:

**The boy's dog was brown.** (One boy owned the dog.)

**The boys' dog was brown.** (More than one boy owned the dog.)

The usual rule for using apostrophes to show that something belong's to someone or something is to put the apostrophe before the *s* if there is one person or thing, and after the *s* if there are more than one.

Many people do'nt understand that apostrophes tell us where there are missing letter's. In *don't* the letter which is missing is the *o* from *do not*, so we put the apostrophe between the *n* and the *t*.

Carrot's
Pea's

Apostrophes, see page 78

# Apostrophes used correctly

▲ All of the apostrophes in this passage are in the right places. Compare it with the one with mistakes and see if you spotted them all.

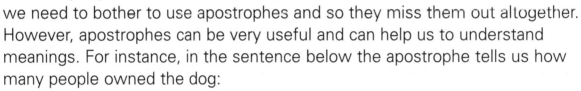

Apostrophes can be found in all sorts of places. It's not unusual to see apostrophes being used in plurals, especially at greengrocers' shops. You often find that carrots, beans, cabbages and peas are on sale. Perhaps the people who write such things think that the words look better with apostrophes!

Some people can't understand why we need to bother to use apostrophes and so they miss them out altogether. However, apostrophes can be very useful and can help us to understand meanings. For instance, in the sentence below the apostrophe tells us how many people owned the dog:

**The boy's dog was brown.** (One boy owned the dog.)
**The boys' dog was brown.** (More than one boy owned the dog.)

The usual rule for using apostrophes to show that something belongs to someone or something is to put the apostrophe before the *s* if there is one person or thing and after the *s* if there are more than one.

Many people don't understand that apostrophes tell us where there are missing letters. In *don't* the letter which is missing is the *o* from *do not*, so we put the apostrophe between the *n* and the *t*.

Changing sentences, see page 80

# Changing statements

Name _____     Date _____

▲ Look at the sentences in the left-hand column and then rewrite them as *questions* and as *negatives*. The first one has been done for you.

| Original sentence | Question | Negative |
|---|---|---|
| Jack had a brand new bicycle. | *Did Jack have a brand new bicycle? OR What did Jack have?* | *Jack did not have a brand new bicycle.* |
| Dogs make very good pets. | | |
| Alice crawled down a rabbit hole. | | |
| Danny hid in the woods with his father. | | |
| Flossie crept into her sister's room. | | |
| Paris is the capital city of France. | | |
| Michael is the best player in the team. | | |
| It is pouring with rain. | | |

Arranging sentences, see page 81

# Family traditions at Christmas (1)

After the turkey we have Christmas pudding and then everyone exchanges presents.

Later in the day we have tea, which is always turkey sandwiches followed by trifle.

When breakfast has been cleared away, we all go to church for the morning service.

Many families have their own traditions for celebrating Christmas.

They bring them into our bedroom to open presents with my wife and me.

Everyone has a stocking in our house.

We have toast and cereal, but no one eats very much because we all know that we have a huge dinner to eat later.

In our house, the day begins very early when the children wake up and find their Christmas stockings.

The church is always packed and everyone is in a good mood.

We eat at 1 o'clock.

Finally, I take the grandparents back to their homes, then come home and go to bed.

My son, Robert, likes to make the gravy and my daughter, Joanne, makes the stuffing for the turkey.

After opening the presents in the stockings, we have breakfast.

When everything is ready to cook and the turkey is in the oven, I go out in the car to pick up all four of the children's grandparents and bring them back for dinner.

While the children play with their gifts, the adults all fall asleep in front of the fire.

The presents in the stockings are usually small and include things like chocolates, fruit, nuts and little games.

In the evening we play games and the adults fall asleep in front of the fire again.

When we get back home, we all help to get the dinner ready by peeling potatoes, chopping carrots and cleaning sprouts.

Arranging sentences, see page 81

# Family traditions at Christmas (2)

Many families have their own traditions for celebrating Christmas. In our house, the day begins very early when the children wake up and find their Christmas stockings. They bring them into our bedroom to open presents with my wife and me. The presents in the stockings are usually small and include things like chocolates, fruit, nuts and little games. Everyone has a stocking in our house.

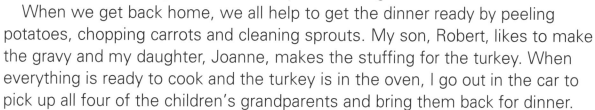

After opening the presents in the stockings, we have breakfast. We have toast and cereal, but no one eats very much because we all know that we have a huge dinner to eat later.

When breakfast has been cleared away, we all go to church for the morning service. The church is always packed and everyone is in a good mood.

When we get back home, we all help to get the dinner ready by peeling potatoes, chopping carrots and cleaning sprouts. My son, Robert, likes to make the gravy and my daughter, Joanne, makes the stuffing for the turkey. When everything is ready to cook and the turkey is in the oven, I go out in the car to pick up all four of the children's grandparents and bring them back for dinner.

We eat at 1 o'clock. After the turkey we have Christmas pudding and then everyone exchanges presents. While the children play with their gifts, the adults all fall asleep in front of the fire.

Later in the day we have tea, which is always turkey sandwiches followed by trifle. In the evening we play games and the adults fall asleep in front of the fire again. Finally, I take the grandparents back to their homes, then come home and go to bed.

# The city of York

York is a nice city. It has many old buildings. Lots of people visit York. It has an old wall which goes almost all the way round the city centre.

The wall has entrances called bars. The bars are called Monk Bar, Bootham Bar, Walmgate Bar and Micklegate Bar. The bars allow people to get in and out of the city.

Many of York's streets are narrow. It can be difficult to walk quickly in York because the streets are so crowded sometimes.

York Minster is a big church. It towers above the rest of the city. You can see it from miles away.

The River Ouse flows through the middle of York. Sometimes it floods parts of the city. Lots of tourists enjoy boat rides on the Ouse.

There are three bridges over the Ouse in the centre of York. They are called Ouse Bridge, Lendal Bridge and Skeldergate Bridge.

There are many interesting places to visit in York. These include York Minster, Jorvik Viking Museum, Castle Museum and Yorkshire Museum. You have to pay to go into the museums. You can still enjoy a visit to York without paying. Many people enjoy simply wandering around the city's narrow streets.

Comparative adjectives, see page 85

# Comparative adjectives

Name _____    Date _____

▲ Complete the sentences using the correct version of the adjectives.

Imogen is the _____ person in the class. (tall)

Mel is _____ at singing than Victoria. (good)

Ewan was _____ than Angus, but Freya was the _____. (fast)

Ben Nevis is the _____ mountain in Scotland. (high)

Ronaldo is the _____ footballer in the world. (good)

Mrs Grant had the _____ car in the whole car park. (old)

Sharifa was the _____ of four children. (young)

Salim had lots of skill but his brother, Imran, was _____.
(skilful)

Mr McNamara thought his baby daughter was the _____
girl in the world. (beautiful)

The _____ river in the United States of America is the Mississippi.
(long)

▲ Make up some more sentences which include the correct versions of these
adjectives: *wonderful, miserable, careless, much* and *generous*. Write them on
the back of the sheet.

Speech marks, see page 86

## Changing reported speech into dialogue

The two friends looked at each other. Sarah said that she had never been so afraid, and Rebecca agreed.

Rebecca told her friend not to worry, and asked her if she would like a piece of chocolate to help keep her spirits up.

Sarah thanked her and took the chocolate, but by the time she had eaten it she had begun to complain of being frightened again. It was two hours since they had seen Rebecca's parents and they were lost, cold and hungry.

Rebecca suggested that they leave the bus shelter and begin to walk home, but Sarah said that that could be dangerous.

Sarah said that she thought a bus would come by soon and they could get on it and make their own way home, but Rebecca pointed out that they had no money for the fare and anyway her parents would probably appear very soon.

Sarah complained that it had been two hours and that Rebecca's parents must surely have forgotten that they were supposed to pick them up at the bus stop.

Suddenly, they saw a car in the distance and listened as the sound of its engine increased as it neared the bus stop. The girls began to jump up and down and shout with relief as Rebecca's mother stopped the car next to the bus stop.

Mrs Dean looked pale and worried and kept apologizing over and over again. She and Mr Dean had been delayed because the car had had two punctures when it ran over some nails on the road. It had taken Mr Dean nearly an hour to walk to a garage and get a mechanic to come and replace one tyre while Mrs Dean had changed the other one.

**128**